797,885 Books

are available to read at

www.ForgottenBooks.com

---◆---

Forgotten Books' App
Available for mobile, tablet & eReader

ISBN 978-1-332-34719-3
PIBN 10317065

This book is a reproduction of an important historical work. Forgotten Books uses
state-of-the-art technology to digitally reconstruct the work, preserving the original format
whilst repairing imperfections present in the aged copy. In rare cases, an imperfection in
the original, such as a blemish or missing page, may be replicated in our edition. We do,
however, repair the vast majority of imperfections successfully; any imperfections that
remain are intentionally left to preserve the state of such historical works.

Forgotten Books is a registered trademark of FB &c Ltd.
Copyright © 2015 FB &c Ltd.
FB &c Ltd, Dalton House, 60 Windsor Avenue, London, SW19 2RR.
Company number 08720141. Registered in England and Wales.

For support please visit www.forgottenbooks.com

1 MONTH OF
FREE
READING

at
www.ForgottenBooks.com

By purchasing this book you are eligible for one month membership to ForgottenBooks.com, giving you unlimited access to our entire collection of over 700,000 titles via our web site and mobile apps.

To claim your free month visit:
www.forgottenbooks.com/free317065

* Offer is valid for 45 days from date of purchase. Terms and conditions apply.

Similar Books Are Available from
www.forgottenbooks.com

How to Handle and Educate Vicious Horses
Together With Hints on the Training and Health of Dogs, by Oscar R. Gleason

Pheasants in Covert and Aviary
by Frank Townend Barton

Pets and How to Care for Them
by Lee S. Crandall

Studies in Horse Breeding
Illustrated Treatise on the Science and Practice of the Breeding of Horses, by G. L. Carlson

Pets for Pleasure and Profit
by Alpheus Hyatt Verrill

Some Pekingese Pets
by M. N. Daniel

Manual of Farm Animals
by Merritt W. Harper

The Aquarium
by Unknown Author

Pets
Their History and Care, by Lee S. Crandall

Man's Best Friend, the Dog
A Treatise Upon the Dog, by George B. Taylor

Concerning Cats
My Own and Some Others, by Helen Maria Winslow

Rabbit and Cat Diseases
by Charles Greatley Saunders

Things Worth Knowing About Horses
by Harry Hieover

The Angora Cat
How to Breed Train and Keep It, by Robert Kent James

Notes on Pet Monkeys and How to Manage Them
by Arthur Henry Patterson

Care and Management of Rabbits
by Chesla Clella Sherlock

Training the Dog
by Robert S. Lemmon

Garden and Aviary Birds of India
by Frank Finn

Biggle Pet Book
by Jacob Biggle

Pets of the Household
Their Care in Health and Disease, by Thomas M. Earl

Practical Queen Rearing

By FRANK C. PELLETT

Associate Editor American Bee Journal, Former State
Apiarist of Iowa, Author of "Productive
Beekeeping" and "Our Backdoor
Neighbors."

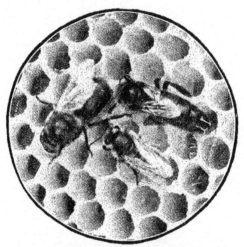

Queen, Drone, and Worker Photographed
from Life. Slightly Enlarged.

Second Edition—Fifth Thousand

AMERICAN BEE JOURNAL,
Hamilton, Illinois.

COPYRIGHT 1918
BY
FRANK C. PELLETT

To my good friend
M. G. DADANT.

Preface

The writer has had the privilege of visiting many of the most extensive queen breeders of America, both north and south, and has tried to present, in the following pages, all the best methods of practice in use in these various apiaries. The book is small, as it has been thought wise to make the descriptions brief and to the point, rather than to elaborate them fully. Beekeepers are usually busy men, and want facts presented as simply and directly as possible in a book of this kind.

The works of Alley, Doolittle, and Sladen have been freely consulted, as well as various texts and bulletins on beekeeping. An effort has been made to make the book worthy of its title, "Practical Queen-Rearing," and methods not of practical value have largely been eliminated.

The illustrations for the most part have appeared in the American Bee Journal, many of them in connection with the author's contributions. A few have been borrowed from other works, as indicated in the text.

Beekeeping has shown a remarkable propensity toward expansion during recent months, the tendency being more and more toward specialization. The demand for good queens has taxed even the most extensive yards to the limit. It is with the hope that the methods here given will prove useful, and that the man of experience, as well as the novice, may find something of value in its pages, that this book is offered to the public.

FRANK C. PELLETT.

Atlantic, Iowa, December 27, 1917.

CONTENTS

Chapter I..9
    Races of Bees.
    Varieties of Mellifica.
    Black or German Bees.
    The Cyprian Bee.
    The Holy-Land Bees or Syrians.
    The Italian Bee.
    Carniolans.
    Caucasians.
    Banat Bees.
    Tunisian or Punic Bees.
    Egyptians.
    Other Races.

Chapter II..19
    Life Story of the Bee.
    Life of the Queen.
    The Drone.
    Queen Rearing in Nature,

Chapter III..23
    Improvement of Stock by Breeding.
    Desirable Traits in Breeding Stock.
    Control of Drones.
    Mating in Confinement a Failure.
    Parthenogenesis.

Chapter IV..31
    Equipment for Queen Rearing.
    Grafting House.
    Mating Hives:
        The Rauchfuss Mating Boxes.
        Baby Nuclei.
        Small Hives.
        Divided Standard Hives.
    Feeders.
    Nursery Cages:
        Alley Nursery Cage.
        Rauchfuss Nursery Cage.
    Shipping Cages.

Chapter V..47
    Early Methods of Queen Rearing:
        Quinby's Method.
        The Alley Plan.

Chapter VI..53
    Present Day Methods of Queen Rearing:
        The Davis Method of Using Drone Comb.
        Natural Built Cells by the Miller Plan.
        Big Batches of Cells by the Case Method
        The Doolittle Cell-cup Method.

Chapter VII 63
    Preparation for Cells:
      Getting Jelly to Start.
      The Author's Plan.
      Transferring the Larvae.

Chapter VIII 71
    Getting Cells Started:
      Removing Queen and Brood.
      The Swarm Box.
      Rearing Queens in Queen-right Colonies.
      Feeding.

Chapter IX 77
    Care of Finished Cells:
      Use of Cell Protectors.
      Formation of Nuclei.
      Stocking Mating Boxes or Baby Nuclei.

Chapter X 83
    Combining Mating with Making of Increase.

Chapter XI 87
    Shipping Queens:
      Making the Candy.
      Caging the Queens.
      What the Buyer has a Right to Expect.
      Grading.

Chapter XII 93
    The Introduction of Queens:
      Details of Cage Methods.
      Direct Introduction.
      Honey and Flour Methods.
      Water Method.
      Introduction of Virgins.

Chapter XIII 101
    The Spread of Disease from the Queen Yard.

INDEX

Page

Albino bees................................13
Alley nursery cage........................44
Alley plan of queen rearing...............49
American bees.............................10
Apis dorsata..............................9
Apis florea...............................9
Apis Indica...............................10
Apis mellifica............................10
Artificial cells..........................60

Baby nuclei............................35—81
Banat bees................................16
Benton queen cage......................44—87
Black bees.............................10—11
Breeder, good traits of...................25
Breeding, to improve stock................23

Cages..............................42—44—87
Cage method of introducing................94
Caging queens.............................88
Candy.....................................87
Case method of queen rearing..............57
Carniolan bees............................15
Cell block.............................55—78
Cell protectors...........................79
Cells care of.............................77
Cells artificial..........................60
Cells preparation for.....................63
Cells starting............................71
Cyprian bees..............................12
Caucasian bees............................16

Davis plan of queen rearing...............53
Davis mating hives................38—40—41
Direct introduction of queens.............96
Disease, spread from queen yards.........101
Doolittle method of queen rearing.........60
Drones....................................20
Drones control of.........................26

Early methods of queen rearing............31
Egyptian bees.............................17
Equipment for queen rearing...............47

Feeders...................................41
Feeding...................................76
Flour method of introducing queens........98
Gentle stock for breeders.................25
German bees............................10—11
Giant bees of India.......................9
Golden bees............................15—26
Grading queens............................89
Grafting...............................65—66
Grafting house............................31
Grafting in drone comb....................53
Grafting tools............................66

Holy land bees............................13
Honey method of introducing queens........98
Hopkins method of queen rearing...........57
Hybrid bees...............................11

Increase, combined with mating............83
Introduction of queens....................93
    Cage method...........................94

Page

Direct methods............................96
Flour method..............................98
Smoke method..............................96
Water method..............................98
Italian bees...........................11—13

Mating:
    In confinement........................28
    Artificial............................28
    In greenhouses........................29
Mating hives......................33—38
Mating-hives, stocking....................81
Miller method of queen rearing............55

Nuclei.................................33—35
    Formation of..........................80
    Baby...............................35—81
Nursery cages..........................42—44

Parthenogenesis...........................29
Present day methods of queen rearing......53
Punic bees................................17

Queen, life of............................19
Queen rearing
    in nature.............................21
    early methods of......................47
    equipment for.........................31
    Alley plan of.........................49
    Davis plan of.........................53
    Case method of........................57
    Hopkins method........................57
    Doolittle method......................60
    Miller method.........................55
    Present day methods...................53
    Quinby's method.......................48
    In queenright colonies................75
Races of bees.............................9
    Albinos...............................13
    Banats................................16
    Blacks.............................10—11
    Carniolans............................15
    Caucasians............................16
    Cyprians..............................12
    Egyptians.............................17
    Goldens............................15—26
    Germans............................10—11
    Holylands.............................13
    Italians...........................11—13
    Punic.................................17
    Syrians...............................13
    Tunisan...............................17
Rauchfuss cage............................44
Rauchfuss mating hive.....................34
Royal jelly...............................63

Shipping cages............................44
Shipping queens...........................87
Stocking mating-hives.....................81
Swarm box..........................40—74

Transferring larvae.......................65

Virgin queens.............................90
    introducing...........................98

ILLUSTRATIONS

Queen, drone and worker .... Title page
Queen cells built under the swarming impulse .... Fig. 1
A large average production is only secured by careful selection .... '' 2
Combs built without foundation contain much drone comb 3
Full sheets of foundation insure worker combs 4
Grafting house in use by southern queen breeders 5
Rauchfuss mating box 6
A baby nucleus at the Minnesota University 7
Small mating hives in the Strong queen yard 8
Mating hives using shallow extracting frames .... '' 9
Eight frame hive adapted for four compartment mating hive ... '' 10
Eight frame hive divided into three parts, with standard frames '' 11
Ten frame hive divided into two parts .... '' 12
Feeding with Mason jars at the Penn yards .... '' 13
The Alley Nursery Cage .... '' 14
The Rauchfuss Nursery Cage .... '' 15
Frame for holding Rauchfuss Cages .... '' 16
Comb cut down for cell-building by Alley plan .... '' 17
Every alternate egg is crushed by Alley plan .... '' 18
Queen cells by Alley plan .... '' 19
Batch of finished cells grafted with drone comb .... '' 20
Cutting away cells built on drone comb .... '' 21
Cell block for handling finished cells .... '' 22
Queen cells built naturally by Miller plan .... '' 23
Frame for holding comb for cell building by Case method ..... '' 24
Frame of prepared cups by Doolittle method .... '' 25
Batch of finished cells by Doolittle method .... '' 26
Larvae not to exceed thirty-six hours of age should be used for
    grafting .... '' 27
Strong colonies should be used for cell-building .... '' 28
Strong cell-finishing colony .... '' 29
Finished cells by the Doolittle method .... '' 30
Method of placing ripe cell in nucleus which has no brood ...... '' 31
Cell protectors .... '' 32
A queen mating yard composed of standard hives .... '' 33
A queen-rearing apiary in Tennessee .... '' 34
Queen mating nuclei under the pine trees of Alabama ...... '' 35
The Benton mailing cage .... '' 36
The Miller introducing cage 37
A Mississippi queen-rearing yard .... '' 38
A Georgia queen-rearing apiary .... '' 39
A queen yard in Minnesota .... '' 40

PRACTICAL QUEEN REARING

CHAPTER I

The Races of Bees.

The family of bees is an extensive one, embracing hundreds of species. On a warm day in spring, one can often see many different kinds of solitary wild bees among the blossoms of the fruit trees. Aside from their usefulness in the pollination of plants, these are of little economic importance. A little higher in the scale we find the bumble bees living together in small families of, at most, a few dozen individuals. In the tropics the stingless bees are still farther advanced in their social organization, and store small quantities of honey which is often taken from them for table use by the inhabitants of the warm countries. However, the amount of honey stored is small compared with the product of a colony of honeybees. While an extended study of the habits of the various species of wild bees would open a fascinating branch of natural history, the genus Apis is the only one that is of practical importance to the honey producer.

Much interest has been manifested in the giant bee of India and Ceylon, *Apis dorsata*, and at one time an attempt was made to introduce it into this country. This bee builds a gigantic comb in the open, usually suspended from a branch of a forest tree. *Dorsata* has a reputation of being very fierce, which Benton denies, saying they are no more so than other bees. Its habit is such that it is very improbable that it could be induced to occupy a hive, because of its single large comb, as our honeybees must do, to be properly managed.

In the east there is another species, *Apis florea*, a gentle little bee, much smaller than the honeybee. It builds a delicate

little comb usually built around a twig. The quality of the
honey is very good and the combs white, but the amount of
honey stored in these diminutive combs is so small that they
can never be of much practical importance, even though it
were possible to induce them to remain in hives, which is very
doubtful.

There is a species in Ceylon and other eastern countries
which has been domesticated with some success, *Apis Indica*. It
is small and excitable, and generally inferior to the European
races. It is known as the common East Indian honeybee.
The natives hive them in small round earthenware pots, later
driving them out with smoke to get the honey. Attempts
to keep them in frame hives of proper dimensions have met with
some success, but the quantity of honey secured is reported
as very discouraging. This species is regarded as a variety
of *mellifica* by some, rather than a distinct species. In any
case it has little claim of interest to the practical beekeeper
who has the better kinds.

Varieties of Mellifica.

All the honeybees known by different names, such as Italians,
Blacks, Carniolans, etc., are now regarded as varieties of one
species, *Apis mellifica*. The differences are such as naturally
result from being bred for long periods of time in particular
environments. Each variety has adapted itself to the particular
conditions under which it lived until it is, very probably, better
adapted to that particular condition, by natural selection, than
any other race or variety would be. Since none of the honeybees are native to America, it can only be determined by trial
which of the varieties is best suited to our conditions. The
Blacks or German bees were first introduced into this country,
and were very generally acclimated in all parts of the United
States, before any other race was introduced. As in many
localities others have since been introduced, a multitude of
crosses, commonly spoken of as hybrids, have resulted. In
localities where no particular attention is paid to the breeding
of bees a new variety which might well be called the American bee

is being developed, as a result of these crosses and the natural adaptation to a new environment. The term "hybrid" is usually used to designate any bee which is not pure, of one race or another. It is quite probable that time will demonstrate that the race which is best suited to the conditions of California is not the best for New York or Minnesota. Up to the present time, the Italians are the only ones which have been given an extended trial in all parts of the country, except the blacks, which were the first to be introduced. There is still room for extensive experiments in comparative tests of the races under the various conditions of different sections of America.

Black or German Bees.*

Black bees are very generally supposed to have been first introduced into America from Germany but very probably they came first from Spain. The native black bees of Great Britain, France, Germany and Spain are said to vary but little. The ground color of the whole body is black with the bands of whitish hairs on the abdomen very narrow and inconspicuous. F. W. L. Sladen, who was at one time extensively engaged in queen rearing in England, says that "In the cool and windy summer climate of the British Isles it is unsurpassed by any other pure race for industry in honey gathering, working early and late."

The blacks are easy to shake off their combs, and cap the comb honey very white, making an attractive product. Since extracted honey is coming more and more into favor, the matter of white capping is of constantly diminishing importance. One of the worst objections to the blacks is their excitable nature. When the hive is opened they run about nervously, and often boil out over the top in a most disconcerting manner. The queens are difficult to find, because of the fact that instead

*"According to the quotations from the American Bee Journal, common bees were imported into Florida, by the Spaniards, previous to 1763, for they were first noticed in West Florida in that year. They appeared in Kentucky in 1780, in New York in 1793, and west of the Mississippi in 1797."—Dadant, *Langstroth on the Honey Bee.*

of remaining quietly on the comb attending to business, they
run with the workers and often hide. They do not gather
as much surplus on the average as Italians, under American
conditions, are more inclined to be cross, and are more suscep-
tible to brood diseases. It is a difficult matter to save an apiary
of black bees, once they become infected with European foulbrood. In comparison with Italians, the latter have proven
so much better that there is a very general tendency to replace
the blacks with Italians and in many limited neighborhoods
where beekeeping is scientifically followed, the blacks have
disappeared.

The Cyprian Bee.

The Cyprian bees are in many respects similar to Italians.
The pure Cyprians are said to be yellow on the sides and under
parts of the abdomen, as well as having the three yellow bands
as do the Italians, but the tip is very black. They are some
what smaller than the Italians, and somewhat more slender
and wasplike in appearance. According to Alley, "The pos-
terior rings of the bodies of the workers are broader than those
of the Italian, and, when examined, it will be noticed that
the upper portion is partially black, terminating on the sides
in a perfect half moon, generally two. It will also be observed
that there is no intermingling of color. With pure Cyprian
bees this is an invariable and uniform marking." They also
have a golden shield between the wings.

The queens are extremely prolific, but the workers are very
cross and not easily subdued by smoke. After extended trial
in America, they have found few friends because of this characteristic. The American beekeeper demands gentle bees.
Aside from the revengeful disposition, they have many good
qualities. They are said to be long lived, to build less drone
comb than other races, to fly farther for stores and to be extremely hardy, wintering well. They continue breeding late in fall,
and are not inclined to dwindle in spring. They build many
queen cells in preparation for swarming, sometimes as many

as a hundred. They defend their stores readily against robbers, and are strong and swift on the wing.

These bees are native to the Island of Cyprus, and were first introduced into this country from Europe. The first direct importation was probably that by D. A. Jones of Ontario, in 1880. It is not probable that pure stock can now be found in this country. It is thought that some strains of the golden Italians have been mixed with Cyprians in developing the bright yellow color.

The Holy-Land Bees, or Syrians.

The Holy-land bees are very similar to the Cyprians in appearance, having the golden shield on the thorax, but they show whiter fuzz rings than either Cyprians or Italians. They were introduced into this country by D. A. Jones at the same time as the Cyprians. These bees are native to Palestine, and are said to be common in the vicinity of Bethlehem, Jerusalem and other Bible cities. While they attracted much attention for a short time following their introduction, they were shortly abandoned and are no longer offered for sale in America, as far as the writer can ascertain. They are said to swarm excessively and to winter poorly, as well as to propolize badly.

THE ALBINOS, formerly popular, are probably of Holy-land origin, mixed with Italian, according to Root. The Albino resembles the Italian in appearance except that the fuzz rings on the abdomen are bright grey or white. Root reports them as decidedly inferior as honey gatherers.

The Italian Bee.

The Italian bee is by far the most popular race in America. It has been tried under all kinds of conditions in all parts of the country with satisfactory results. It is resistant to wax moth and European foulbrood, a good honey gatherer and gentler than the black race which preceded it.

This race was first introduced into this country from Italy.

The story of the first importations is told by Mr. Richard Colvin of Baltimore, in the Report of the Secretary of the U. S. Department of Agriculture for 1863, as follows:

The first attempt to import the Italian honey-bee into the United States, it is believed, was made about the year 1855 by Messrs. Samuel Wagner and Edward Jessup, of York, Pennsylvania; but in consequence of inadequate provision for their safety on so long a voyage, they perished before their arrival.

In the winter of 1858-59 another attempt was made by Mr. Wagner, Rev. L. L. Langstroth and myself. The order was placed in the hands of the surgeon of the steamer (to whose charge the bees were to have been committed on the return voyage), with instructions to transmit it to Mr. Dzierzon on reaching Liverpool; but in consequence of his determining to leave the ship to engage in other service on his arrival at Bremen, it was not done and the effort failed. Subsequently arrangements were made by which, in the latter part of that year, we received seven living queens. At the same time, and on board the same steamer, Mr. P. J. Mahan, of Philadelphia, brought one or more queens, which were supposed to be of doubtful purity. Only two or three young queens were reared by us during that fall and winter, and in the following spring we found all our imported stock had perished.

In conjunction with Mr. Wagner I determined to make another trial, and another order was immediately dispatched. The queens, however, did not arrive until the following June. Meantime, about the month of May, Mr. S. B. Parsons, of Flushing, Long Island, received an importation of them from the northern part of Italy, some of the progeny of which he placed in the hands of the Rev. L. L. Langstroth, Mr. W. W. Carey, Mr. M. Quinby, and other skilful apiarians, who with Mr. C. W. Rose, a subsequent importer, and perhaps some others, have bred and disseminated them pretty widely through our country."

There was much interest in the new race, and, for a long time, queens commanded from ten to twenty dollars each in some cases. The late Charles Dadant was one of the early breeders, who imported stock from Italy direct.

The Italian has been bred in America on such an extensive scale that various strains have been developed. The so-called three banded or leather colored Italians are probably more nearly typical than the goldens or five banded Italians. The Italian bee from northern Italy has three yellow bands, with pronounced bands of whitish or grey hair on each of the segments except the first and the last. It is a mild tempered bee, usually being gentle and quiet under manipulation. Unlike the blacks these bees cling closely to their combs, and the queen will often continue her egg laying when the comb on which she is working is removed from the hive and held up to the light.

It is a prolific race, and stands extremes of temperature very well. It winters well and is not adversely affected by the heat of the dry summers of the central west. The beekeeper who does not care to experiment will do well to stick to the Italians, at least until other races have been given more extended tests than have so far been given. While there are a few warm advocates of Caucasians and Carniolans, by far the greater number of practical beekeepers contend that the Italians are the best race. It is only fair to state, however, that no other race has been given the same opportunity to demonstrate its good points, and it is altogether probable that some other race may yet prove best adapted for certain climatic conditions.

THE GOLDENS, are the result of special breeding by selecting the queens whose progeny show the brightest color. It is thought that some strains of goldens are somewhat mixed with the Cyprians, from which ancestry came the bright color. Some breeders have paid so much attention to selecting the brightest colored individuals, regardless of other traits, that some strains are unduly cross, are poor honey gatherers and are not considered hardy. On the other hand there are strains which have been selected with due care to retain other desirable traits along with the bright color, which are gentle and productive.

Carniolans.

The Carniolans resemble the blacks but are larger, the abdomens are of a more bluish cast and the abdominal rings are more distinct. They have the reputation of being excessive swarmers, although the queens are extremely prolific. They are a gentle race and reported to be good honey gatherers, and to stand extremely cold winters. Because of their excessive swarming tendency, they are not popular with American bee-keepers, but the dark color is sufficient in itself to condemn them with many who admire the bright colored bees.

It is important that they be given a fair trial in northern sections, with a hive adapted to discourage swarming, by giving plenty of room for the extremely prolific queens. The Dadant hive or Langstroth frames of jumbo depth are best suited for this purpose of any hive in the market. Since they winter well and the colonies are inclined to be populous, it would seem that they should be especially adapted to extracted honey production in colder latitudes, if the swarming tendency can be overcome.

This race is native to the province of Carniola, Austria, and was first brought to this country in the eighties. It is said that there is much variation in the markings of the bees in the province from which they came. They deposit very little propolis, and are quiet on the combs during manipulation, two desirable traits.

Caucasians.

The Caucasians greatly resemble the blacks in appearance, but they are very different in disposition. They are said to be the gentlest race of bees known. The most serious objection to them is the fact that they deposit propolis freely, being the opposite of Carniolans in this respect. They swarm freely and build quantities of burr and brace combs, which is a source of annoyance to the beekeeper. They have many desirable traits, wintering well, capping their honey white and not being inclined to drift into the hives of other colonies than their own. Since they resemble the blacks so closely, it is next to impossible to tell whether or not they are pure, which is a serious drawback to the careful breeder. A few who have tried them extensively are warm in their praises of the Caucasians and contend that they are superior to the Italians. While this may be doubted, they are worthy of a more general trial than they have so far received. A few breeders now offer queens for sale.

Banat Bees.

The Banats come from Hungary and greatly resemble the Carniolans. Some contend that they are not distinct. They are very gentle, dark in color and very prolific. They build up rapidly in spring and are said to be less inclined to swarm than the Carniolans.

Mr. T. W. Livingstone of Leslie, Georgia, had Banats, exclusively, in his apiaries and regarded them highly. He reported them as very gentle, building up early in spring and rearing brood all season.

Tunisian or Punic Bees.

This is a black race coming from the north coast of Africa. Although given a trial in America they did not meet with favor and none are now present in this country so far as known. They are bad propolizers, extremely cross, and do not winter well. They seem to have been lately given a trial in Scotland. Mr. John Anderson of the North Scotland College of Agriculture, writing in the Irish Bee Journal, October, 1917, says of them that they have some very desirable characteristics, and some that are inconvenient. He mentions the case of a beekeeper who depends solely on honey production for a livelihood (which is unusual in Great Britain), who increased forty colonies to four hundred and harvested two-and-one-half tons of honey in one season without feeding any sugar. Mr. Anderson regards the Punic bee as worthy of more attention than it has received.

Egyptians.

Bees have been kept in a primitive way for centuries in Egypt. The Egyptian bees resemble Italians in color, with an additional coat of white hairs. They are said to breed purely and not be inclined to mate with other races. They are somewhat smaller than the European races, and build somewhat smaller cells in their combs. They are reported to be cross and not easily subdued by smoke. Since they do not form a winter cluster, they are not fitted to withstand severe weather. They are said to rear large numbers of drones, and to develop fertile workers in abundance. They are not likely to prove of any value in America. In fact, they were introduced soon after the Civil War, but either perished from cold or were abandoned in favor of more promising races.

Other Races.

There are numerous other races in Asia and Africa which are as yet but little known in this country. It is hardly probable that new races superior to those already introduced will be found. The native Grecian bee is said to resemble the hybrids so common in this country, but has probably not been tried here as yet.

CHAPTER II

Life Story of the Bee.

In a normal colony of bees, during the summer season, will be found one queen, several thousand workers and a few dozen drones. If the bees are left to themselves and receive no attention from their owner, the number of drones is greatly increased, and often reaches the point where they consume what might otherwise be stored as surplus honey. Since there are but few readers of a book of this nature who are not already familiar with the life of the honeybee, it would seem, at first thought, that little space need be occupied in consideration of this subject. However, the volume cannot be complete without some attention to the life history of the insects, especially with attention to those points with special bearing on the subject of queen rearing.

Since the life of the colony centers in the queen, she becomes of special importance, and she receives attention from the workers worthy of her special place. Should she be removed from the hive, great excitement will shortly prevail with manifestation of serious distress on the part of the inmates. Unless she be promptly returned, the bees will prepare to replace her by starting numerous queen cells, utilizing the newly hatched larvae for the purpose.

Life of the Queen.

As stated elsewhere, all fertilized eggs laid by the queen produce female offspring. Whether these shall develop as queens or workers is determined by the environment in which the development takes place. In any case the egg hatches in about three days. Where eggs are placed in queen cells it is very doubtful whether they receive any different treatment before hatching than do the eggs in ordinary worker cells. It is after the hatching of the egg that the embryo queen receives special attention, which results in the perfect development of her sexual organs. The larger cell in which she finds herself, together with a plenteous supply of the rich food known as royal jelly, makes of her a very different creature than of her sister in the worker cell.

The queen lacks the wax secreting organs as well as the pollen baskets of the worker. Neither has she the same highly developed eyes as the worker. Her period of development is much shorter, while her body is larger and quite different in appearance. Approximately sixteen days are necessary for the complete development of the queen bee from the time of the laying of the egg. Of this, three days are necessary for the egg to hatch, six days are spent in the larval stage, and seven days in completing the final transformation, during which she is sealed up in the cell. Twelve days are necessary for the last stage of development of the worker, thus requiring twenty-one days for the entire development.

Apparently the queen larvae are fed for the first thirty-six hours in very similar manner to the workers. After that time they are fed far more of the royal jelly than they can possibly consume, being left to float in the rich white substance. While the worker is fed on pollen and honey during the latter part of her period of development, the queen larvae is fed the royal jelly during the entire period of larval growth.

The Drone.

The drones are male bees and, apparently, serve no other purpose than the perpetuation of the species. Since under normal conditions a queen bee mates but once in her lifetime, but few drones are needed to serve the purpose for which they are designed by nature. In a state of nature, where colonies are isolated it may be needful that a large number of drones be reared to insure that the young queen will meet one when she goes forth to her mating flight. Where dozens of hives are kept together in a single apiary, as is the case in practice of commerical beekeeping, the beekeeper may keep the number down to the minimum, without danger that a sufficient number will not be present. Hundreds of apiaries are unprofitable because their owners fail to take the necessary care to insure the reduction of the number of drones, which consume the surplus of the colony instead of adding to the store.

Except in the case of the queen breeder who wishes to propagate large numbers of males from choice colonies for breeding purposes, the presence of an over-abundance of drones is a serious handicap to the success of the beekeeper. The use of full sheets of foundation in the brood frames is the best insurance against the raising of drones.

The cells in which drones are reared are similar in appearance to worker cells, except that they are larger in size. They are utilized for the storage of honey the same as are the worker cells. When the brood is developing the high arched cappings, like rifle bullets, will instantly distinguish them from the smooth capping of worker brood. Twenty-five days is necessary for the development of the drone from the time the egg is laid until it reaches maturity. Mating of honeybees takes place on the wing, and the act is fatal to the drone. He dies almost instantly, and his sexual organs are torn from his body and borne away attached to the body of the queen. After all the seminal fluid has been absorbed by the queen, the parts are removed, apparently by the workers which can sometimes be seen pulling at them after the return of the queen.

Queen Rearing in Nature.

Under normal conditions the bees build queen cells on two occasions, to supersede the old queen or in preparation for swarming. Where the old queen shows signs of failing, the bees will often build only one or two cells. When the young queen emerges, she will often be mated and begin laying without manifesting any antagonism toward the old queen. It thus happens that the beekeeper frequently will find two lay-

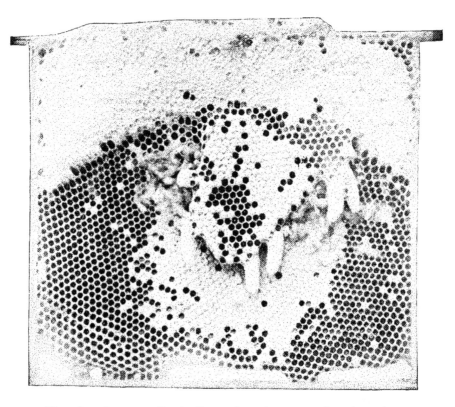

Fig. 1. Queen cells built under the swarming impulse.

ing queens in the old hive. It is usually but a short time until the old one will disappear. As soon as the first virgin emerges she will at once seek out any other queen cells which may be present and destroy the occupants, unless prevented from doing so by the workers, as is the case when there is preparation for swarming.

When swarming is in prospect several cells are usually built, and the number may be twenty or more at the height of the season. With some other races the number is much greater than with the Italians.

The beekeeper with a few colonies can sometimes supply his needs by simply cutting out the surplus cells, built in anticipation of swarming, and using them to replace undesirable queens, or in the making of increase.

CHAPTER III

Improvement of Stock by Breeding.

It is highly important that every person engaged in commercial queen rearing, should make a careful study of the laws of breeding, and make a conscientious effort to improve his stock. Marvelous results have come from careful breeding of live stock and poultry, and even more striking results have attended the efforts of the painstaking plant breeders. Since bees are subject to the same laws of heredity, there is no reason why they cannot be likewise improved if the same care is given to the selection and mating of queens, that is given to other animals.

Fig. 2. A large average production is only secured by careful attention to the selection of stock.

The fact that there is great difficulty in controlling the male parentage, makes the problem of breeding bees a more serious one than breeders of animals have to face.   On the other hand, the possibility of several succeeding generations in a single season makes it possible to secure results in a much shorter period of time.

The beekeeper, who is intent on bettering his stock, finds it much simpler to replace his poor stock with a better grade than does the farmer who has a herd of scrub cattle or sheep. Simply replacing the queens in his colonies shortly has the effect of changing the entire stock in the apiary, since the workers are short lived.   If he is not inclined to buy enough queens to replace the poorer ones in all his hives, he can very shortly rear enough on his own account to do so, if he will give the matter a little attention. If he buys even one good queen, he can shortly improve the entire stock of an apiary of one hundred or more colonies. To do this he should rear as many young queens as there are colonies in his apiary, and use them to replace the old and inferior queens. If he does this early in the season, he need give little thought to the mating of his young queens. If the mother from which he rears his stock is pure, all the young queens will be pure. To be sure, most of them will be mated with inferior drones, but it is a well known fact that it is only the female offspring that are affected by the mating of a queen. If her mother is purely mated, all her drones will be pure, regardless of her own mating. Within a few weeks there will be thousands of pure drones, the offspring of the young queens that have been introduced. The beekeeper should then rear a second lot of queens from a pure mother to replace all the mismated ones which were introduced early in the season. By this time, most of the drones present will be pure, and the second lot of queens will mostly be purely mated. It is thus a simple matter to replace the entire stock of a neighborhood with pure bees from the offspring of a single pure queen.

Desirable Traits in Breeding Stock.

No queen should be used as a breeder unless she is prolific, since this is of the first importance in determining the amount of honey stored. However, it is not always the most prolific colonies which store the most honey. Longevity of the bees is an important consideration, and quite possibly the difference in length of the tongues of the workers may have an important influence. It often happens that in a poor season a single colony will store a good crop, when others equally strong will get but little, or even require to be fed. The author had one such colony which made a remarkable showing for three successive seasons. The difference in production was so marked that most of the young queens reared were from this queen. A measurement of the length of the tongues of her workers showed that they possessed a slightly longer tongue than others in the apiary, or even other apiaries where measurements were made in comparison. Increased length of the tongues of the workers would place much nectar within their reach, which would otherwise be denied them. It is well worth while to have careful measurements of tongues of all colonies which make unusual showing, under adverse conditions.

In general, the breeder selects queens for breeding from colonies which store the most surplus, with little enquiry as to the particular reason therefor. Since honey is the principal desideratum of the beekeeper, he is not so much concerned in the reason why a special colony stores more, as he is in finding the particular colony.

Next to production, gentleness is a most important characteristic. It is very disagreeable to have bees that meet one half way to begin the day's work, and follow one about constantly. The fear of stings is the principal objection to beekeeping on the part of many people. While stings can largely be prevented by suitable protection in the way of veils and gloves, it is far better to select gentle stocks for breeding purposes. Where only the gentle colonies are selected for breeding stock, it is possible to very largely reduce the annoyance of stinging.

It would seem to be possible to select gentle colonies which are also good producers, and, at the same time, have other desirable characteristics.

Color should be a secondary consideration, although it is desirable to have bees nicely marked. For a time, so much attention was paid to color on the part of breeders of Italians, that everything else was sacrificed in order to get yellow bees. This was carried to such an extreme that a very general prejudice has grown up against the Goldens.   While it is quite true that some strains of the Goldens are not desirable, being neither hardy nor good honey gatherers, there are strains where proper attention has been given to other points, which are very satis-factory.   In general, the Goldens have a bad reputation for being ugly in disposition, yet at least one strain of Goldens is very gentle. Very much depends upon the queen breeder, and the care he uses in selecting his breeding stock.   Some breed-ers go so far as never to use a queen for a breeder, unless the colony can be handled under normal conditions without smoke.

The non-swarming propensity is also to be favored.   In many localities the honeyflows are short, and, if the colony swarms at the beginning of the flow, there is little chance of harvesting a good crop.   Too much care cannot be used in selecting the colonies to use for breeders.   Much more attention is given to selecting the queen from whose offspring the young queens are to be reared, than is given to the parentage of the drones.   The confession must be made that few breeders give any special attention to this point, although it is equally as important as far as practical results are concerned.

Control of Drones.

Since the queen is mated on the wing, and there is always the possibility that the young queen will meet an inferior drone from a distance, it is highly important that a queen breeder go to a good deal of trouble to insure that all bees within a radius of five miles of his breeding yards are requeened with pure stock of the race which he is breeding.   Unless he takes this precaution, there will be much dissatisfaction on the part of his customers from receiving mismated queens.

If a breeder is so fortunate as to be within reach of a suitable place to establish a mating station where no other bees are within reach, he can do much to improve the quality of his stock. Under such circumstances, he can select his drones with the same care that he selects the mother of his queens. A colony combining as many as possible of the desirable characteristics can be carried to the isolated position where the matings are to be made and left there. A few have undertaken to rear queens on islands where no other bees are present. The broad prairies of several states offer similar isolation.

Fig. 3. Combs built on starters only or without foundation contain a large percentage of drone cells and result in unprofitable colonies.

Unfortunately, however, few breeders are so situated that they can control the drones thus completely. After requeening all the bees within flying distance of the apiary, the next thing is to select the best colonies as drone breeders and supply them with an abundance of drone comb. This insures that large numbers of drones will fly from these colonies, and thus increase the chances that young queens will meet desirable mates.   Care should be used to make sure that the combs in the brood nests of other colonies than the breeders contain as little drone comb as possible, and thus reduce the production of drones to the lowest possible minimum.   Traps may be used

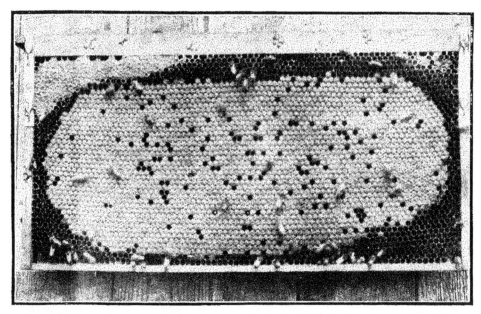

Fig. 4. Full sheets of foundation in the brood frames insure worker combs and a minimum of drone production.

also to catch such drones as appear in undesirable colonies. Unless the breeder is willing to go to great length to control his breeding stock and thus give his customers the best which it is possible for him to produce, he should by all means confine his attention to the production of honey or some other business.   There are entirely too many indifferent queen breeders for the good of the industry.

Mating in Confinement a Failure.

Some practical method of absolute control of mating has long been sought. At the University of Minnesota Prof. Jager succeeded in getting one queen impregnated artifically and for a time it was hoped that enough queens could be mated in this way for use in breeding experiments. However, after numerous trials on the part of Prof. Jager, C. W. Howard, and L. V. France, at the University, no further successful instances have been reported.

The A. I. Root Company tried some rather elaborate experiments in getting queens mated in large greenhouses, but these were likewise a failure. While enthusiasts have claimed success at different times by one method or another, their claims have generally been discredited, and up to the present, there seems little prospect of artificial control of the mating. About all that now seems possible, is to select isolated situations for the mating stations, or to limit the breeding of drones as far as possible in undesirable colonies, and encourage it in the colonies from which it is desirable to breed.

Parthenogenesis.

When the discovery was first made that unimpregnated females often are capable of producing male offspring, the public was slow to accept the fact. There was much discussion of the subject for years before it was finally accepted as a settled fact, rather common among insects. It is now well known among beekeepers that queens which fail to mate will sometimes lay a considerable number of eggs which will hatch, but all will be drones. In the same manner fertile workers produce drones which are usually smaller in size and inferior in appearance, but some very careful observers are of the opinion that they are quite capable of mating in the normal manner.

Since the mating of a queen has no direct effect on her male offspring, her workers may be hybrids, and her drones pure. It is hardly within the scope of this little book to go into detail concerning the proof of such well established facts as those above stated. These may be found in detail in several of the old text books. Those who are interested in pursuing the subject further are referred to Dadant's revision of Langstroth on the Honeybee, where a full account of the various experiments along this line are given.

The thing that we are concerned with just now is the practical effect that the facts may have upon the problems of the queen breeder, and these we have set out as briefly as possible in the foregoing pages.

CHAPTER IV

Equipment for Queen Rearing.

The kind and amount of equipment necessary for queen rearing will depend to a great extent upon conditions. The beekeeper who wishes to rear but a few queens for use in requeening his own apiaries, can get along very well with limited equipment. The commercial queen breeder, who expects to send out several thousand queens each year, will do well to provide a liberal amount of equipment, for, otherwise, he will be hampered and unable to get the best results. An effort is made here to describe the various systems of management, and the reader can select what most appeals to him. In general, the simpler the system, the more efficient and the larger the amount of work which can be accomplished in a given time. Several different methods are described for doing the same thing, yet it is manifestly unwise for any individual to provide himself with all the equipment described, or to undertake the various systems outlined, unless it be for the purpose of experiment rather than for practical results. Usually it is best to use modifications of equipment used for commercial honey production so that in the event of a change back to regular beekeeping the equipment can mostly be used, or sold to other beekeepers in case of giving up the work. Second hand queen-rearing equipment is difficult to sell, since there are comparatively few men engaged in commercial queen rearing.

Grafting House.

On visiting the queen breeders of the south, I was much impressed with a grafting house in common use in the queen rearing apiaries of Alabama. While it is possible to make use of the kitchen or other warm room in the house, or to do the work in the open air in warm weather, the little building

Fig. 5.   Grafting house in use by southern queen breeders.

shown at Figure 5 is far more desirable.   As will be seen in
the picture, the building is made of matched lumber and is
very tight.   A seat is provided for the operator, and in front
of it a bench or table running across the building and about
two feet wide.   This provides ample room for combs, tools,
etc., and one can work in comfort and at leisure.   The entire
front above the table is composed of window sash, thus providing
an abundance of light.   Some of these grafting houses, like the
one shown, are also provided with glass in the roof like a photog-
rapher's studio.   It is well to provide a shutter to cover the
roof in extremely hot weather, or to protect the glass during
storms.   A shade is also desirable for the front, to shut out too
much sunlight at times.   A room four by six feet is amply
large for this purpose, and, by means of a small oil stove, it
can be kept warm in cool weather.   This is important to prevent the chilling of the larvae while grafting.   Some of the
more extensive queen breeders find it necessary to graft cells

every day during the season, rain or shine, and during the rush days of midsummer must prepare hundreds of cells.   Not the least of the advantages of this building is the protection from robbers.   Where it is necessary for the operator to be at work for several hours at a time, this little building in the center of the yard is a great time and labor saver, as well as adding much to the convenience and comfort of the operator.   It merits more general use.   While the one shown in the picture admits more light than is necessary on bright days, the extra glass space will be much appreciated in dark and cloudy weather.

Mating-Hives.

The honey producer who rears queens only for the purpose of improving his stock or requeening his apiaries, seldom both ers much about mating-hives.   When he has a lot of sealed cells ready for use, he simply kills off the old queens to be replaced and about twenty-four hours later gives each of the colonies a sealed cell.   In this way he avoids the bother of introducing queens, for the young queen will emerge in the hive where she is expected to remain.   From there she will take her mating flight, and, the only further concern necessary on the part of the beekeeper, is to take care to replace any queens that are lost on their nuptial flight or that fail to emerge properly.

The commercial queen breeder will require a large number of nuclei or small colonies to care for surplus queens, until they are mated and ready to be mailed to customers.   There is a large variety of hives of various sizes used for this purpose. Where queen breeding is the prime object, the tendency is to use as small hives and as few bees as possible, so that the largest possible number of queens may be reared with the bees and equipment available.   However, many of the most success- ful queen breeders find serious objections to baby nuclei and small mating boxes, and advocate nothing but standard frames for mating-hives.

The beekeeper should provide the box with a piece of queen excluding zinc which

The Rauchfuss Mating Boxes.

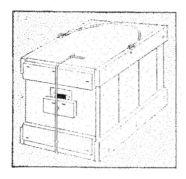

Fig. 6.
Rauchfuss Mating Box.

This is perhaps the smallest mating box ever devised which has been used successfully. Beginners or those with limited experience, are quite likely to have much difficulty from the bees swarming out to accompany the queen on her mating flight with any small nucleus. Even the most expert are never able to overcome this difficulty entirely.

The Rauchfuss nucleus consists of a small box with removable front, holding three 4¼x4¼ comb-honey sections, Figure 6. The entrance is by means of a small round hole in the front, which can be closed entirely, when moving them, by simply turning a small button. As devised by the inventor, one section of sealed honey is used, and sealed brood is removed from a strong colony and cut into squares of the right size to fill one of the remaining sections. The presence of the brood will in many cases prevent the bees from absconding when the queen takes her flight. When used without the brood, there will be a larger percentage of loss from absconding. A cupful of young bees taken from a strong colony is sufficient to stock the box, when a virgin queen from a nursery cage is run in through the entrance hole. After the box is stocked and the young queen run in, the entrance is stopped. When all boxes to be stocked at one time are ready, all are carried to a point some distance from the apiary and tied in trees, set on some convenient object, or otherwise placed until the queens shall be mated. Of course the entrance should be opened as soon as conditions are favorable after reaching the destination. It will be necessary to remove the queens from these diminutive hives soon after they begin to lay. Should it be inconvenient to do so at once, the box is provided with a piece of queen excluding zinc which can be turned over the entrance hole, thus preventing the queen from escaping, while permitting the bees to go afield.

The great advantage of this mating box is the small first cost, and the small number of bees necessary to stock the nucleus. They are listed at about forty cents each in lots of ten.

Baby Nuclei.

The Root baby nucleus which is quite generally used is a small double hive, each side containing two frames 5⅝x8 inches in size. Three of these little frames will just fill a standard Langstroth frame, and to get combs built in them it is necessary to put them in Langstroth frames, and insert them in strong colonies of bees. Some cut up combs and fit them into the little frames. Entrances to the two compartments are at opposite

Fig. 7. A baby nucleus at the Minnesota University queen-rearing station.

ends of the box. About a half a pint of bees is used to stock each compartment. This, in effect, is very similar to the Rauchfuss mating box, excepting that it is necessary to go to more trouble to get combs built especially for these nuclei. There is the same trouble from absconding, and the same danger of being robbed by strong colonies if left within reach. During a good honey flow when all conditions are favorable, it is possible to get a large number of queens mated in these little hives with a minimum of cost in bees, but during a dearth when it becomes necessary to feed to keep any kind of nucleus from going to pieces, they are likely to prove the source of much annoyance. See Figure 7.

Small Hives.

At Figure 8, we show some small hives formerly popular with queen breeders, but which have almost gone out of use. As will be seen in the picture, one is single and the other is double. The double one has entrances opening in opposite directions to avoid danger of the queen entering the wrong compartment.

Fig. 8.   Small mating hives in Strong queen yard.   This type of hive was
once quite generally used but is now going out of use.
[From Productive Beekeeping.]

These little hives hold three, and sometimes four, small frames. They are large enough to hold a nice little cluster of bees, and once established they can sustain themselves very nicely under favorable conditions. Mr. J. L. Strong, formerly extensively engaged in queen rearing in Iowa, used these mating hives for about twenty-five years with satisfaction. However, since the frame is an odd size, it is necessary either to cut up combs and fit into them, or get them built in the nucleus, so there is sometimes difficulty in getting them properly fitted out to begin with. There is really nothing to be said for them in preference to a standard hive divided into two or three compartments, and the latter can be used for any other purpose as well.

A few queen breeders use a shallow nucleus which is of the same length as the standard hive. In this they use shallow extracting frames. Although the frames are of the same size

Fig. 9. Mating hives using shallow extracting frames. Achord queen yards in Alabama.

as those used in the apiary, the top, bottom and body must be
made especially.   Nuclei of this type as used by W. D. Achord,
of Alabama, are shown at Figure 9.   Instead of the usual hive
record, short pieces of different colors are placed at the front
end of the cover.   The position of these pieces, which can be
moved to any position at will, indicate the conditions within
the hive.

Divided Standard Hives.

Fig. 10.   Langstroth   hive body
adapted for four-compartment mating
hive, used by J. M. Davis of Tennessee.

By far the greater
number of queen breeders
use the standard Langs-
troth hive, divided into
two or more parts. J. M.
Davis, of Tennessee, di-
vides the ordinary hive
into four parts. This
makes use of standard
hive bodies, tops and bot-
toms, but requires a spe-
cial frame as shown in
Figure 10. The two di-
vision boards that are running lengthwise are easily
removed, thus leaving the
hive in only two parts.
In this way it is possible
to unite two of the clus-
ters at the close of the
season, and leave them
strong enough for winter-
ing in that mild climate.
There is an entrance at
each of the four corners,
each facing in a different
direction. The four com-
partments are lettered A,

B, C, and D.   In opening the hive he makes it a point always
to begin at A and examine each division in regular order to
avoid overlooking any one of them.

At the apiary of Prof. Francis Jager where the queen breeding work of the State of Minnesota is carried on, an eight frame
hive is divided into three parts, each part taking two standard
frames.   There is one entrance at each side, and one at an end.
All that is necessary to make an eight frame hive into three
nuclei, is to have two tight fitting division boards which fit
into sawed slots at the ends.   These must reach to the bottom
to prevent the mixing of bees or the queens from passing from
one compartment to another.   It is necessary of course to fit
the bottom board for the special purpose with entrance openings
in the proper place.   Our illustration (Figure 11) shows a small
cover just the right size to cover one of the three compartments.

Fig. 11. Eight-frame hive divided into three parts; each with two standard frames, at the Jager apiary.

This is placed over the middle division when the regular cover is removed, to prevent the mixing of bees while the hive is open.

Fig. 12.   Ten-frame hive divided into two parts as used for mating hives by Ben G. Davis of Tennessee.

Both the eight and ten frame hives arranged in this manner are in general use.

Ben G. Davis, of Tennessee, the well known breeder of Goldens, is an advocate of strong nuclei which are capable of passing through a dearth or other unfavorable season without much fussing on the part of the queen breeder. With five hundred or a thousand weaklings, the queen breeder finds it a very difficult matter to carry on operations under adverse conditions. Mr. Davis feels that the extra cost of these stronger nuclei is cheap insurance against a poor season. Figure 12 shows his big nuclei, where a ten frame hive is divided into two parts, each with four frames. These nuclei are strong enough to store sufficient honey to winter them successfully under normal conditions, and the time saved from fussing with daily feeding and constant attention more than repays the larger investment. Then there is no trouble whatever in stocking nuclei formed in this manner. All that is necessary in order to increase the number, is to remove one or two frames of emerging brood from a strong colony, for each nucleus, give them a queen or ripe cell and let them build up slowly during the summer, as one young queen after another is mated and permitted to begin laying.

Feeders.

Some kind of feeder will be necessary to stimulate the cell-starting and cell-building colonies, at such times as no honey is coming from the field. If small nuclei are used, it will often become necessary to feed them as well. Since nearly every apiary is provided with feeders of one kind or another, it hardly seems important in a work like this to enter into a discussion of the different types of feeders in the market, and the special merits of each. The Doolittle division board feeder is very popular among queen breeders, as is also the Alexander bottom feeder. However, practically every type of feeder now in the market is in use somewhere in a queen-breeding apiary. The Penn Company, of Mississippi, use a Mason jar with small holes in the metal cover. This is inverted in a round hole in

the center of the cover of the hive, Figure 13.   In passing through
the yard, one can see at a glance the exact amount of feed available to every colony.   The feeders are easily filled and replaced
without opening the hives, and, at the same time, place the feed
above the cluster.

Nursery Cages.

During much of the season a queen breeder with an active
trade will have no use for nursery cages.   Each cell will be placed
in a nucleus a day or two before time for the queen to emerge,
and there she will remain until removed to fill an order to requeen a colony.   However, it often happens that a batch of
cells will mature when no queenless nuclei are ready to receive
them, and it becomes necessary to care for them otherwise

Fig. 13.   Feeding with Mason jars set in the top of hives at the Penn
Company yards.

for a day or two, until room can be made for them. Then some breeders make a practice of allowing the young queens to emerge in the nursery cages before placing them in the nuclei. In this case, cages will be necessary.

There is a considerable percentage of loss when queens are permitted to remain several days in the cage. Some will creep back into the cell and be unable to back out again, while others will die from other causes. Sometimes, the bees will feed them through the wire cloth, but this is not to be depended upon, and the cages must be stocked with candy to insure plenty of feed within reach. Doolittle advocates smearing a drop of honey on the small end of the cell when placing it in the nursery, in order to provide the queen with her first meal as soon as she cuts the capping of the cell. Candy is also provided to furnish food in sufficient quantity during the period that she is confined in the cage. The cages must be kept warm, of course, while the cells are incubating, and for this purpose they are usually left hanging in the hive with a strong colony. However, the bees will not keep the cells in cages sufficiently warm after the weather gets cool in late fall, nor in early spring. At such times it becomes necessary to provide a nursery heated with a lamp or other artificial heat, in which the frames of nursery cages can be hung.

Some queen breeders utilize an ordinary poultry incubator for this purpose, maintaining it at the normal hive temperature.

E. B. Ault of Texas has fitted up an outdoor cellar with artificial heat for the purpose of incubating his sealed queen cells.

Alley Nursery Cage.

Fig. 14.
The Alley nursery cage.

The Alley cage, Figure 14, is the most popular cage, although this may be because it has been so long on the market.   A nursery frame is offered by supply houses which holds twenty four of these cages.   The larger hole is just the right size to take a cell built on a cell block.   The block makes an effective stopper for the hole after the emergence of the young queen.   Candy for provision is placed in the smaller hole.

Rauchfuss Nursery Cage.

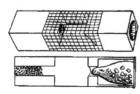

Fig. 15. The Rauch-fuss combined nursery and introducing cage.

The Rauchfuss cage has not been long in the market, but bids fair to come into general use.   Figure 15 shows the cage and Figure 16 the frame to hold about three dozen of them.   This cage can be used for any purpose for which a cage is needed about the apiary.   The hole at one end is large enough to take a ripe cell, while the candy at the other end can be eaten away, thus releasing the queen, and making it a desirable introducing cage.

Shipping Cages.

The Benton mailing cage has come into almost universal use among queen breeders.   This is used as a combined mailing and introducing cage.   It has been found that a small cage is desirable for sending queens in the mail, as there is less danger of injury when thrown about in the mailsacks than in a larger cage where there is more room to be bumped about.   When larger cages are used, where the queen and her escort must

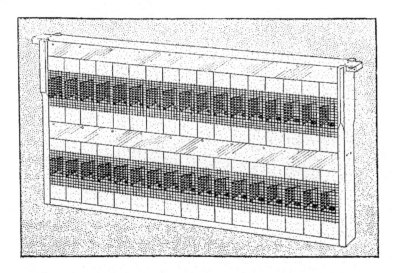

Fig. 16. Frame for holding Rauchfuss nursery cages.

travel long distances, as for export trade, a correspondingly larger number of bees are enclosed, thus saving each other from the shocks incident to travel through the mails.

Minor Equipment, such as cell blocks, cell protectors, etc., will be taken up in connection with the chapters relating to their use.

CHAPTER V

Early Methods of Queen Rearing.

Prior to the invention of the movable frame hive little progress was made in the development of beekeeping. Commercial queen rearing as now practiced has been developed within the memory of our older beekeepers. As soon as his invention of the loose frames made the control of conditions within the hive possible, Langstroth began to experiment in the hope of being able to control natural swarming, and make necessary increase at his convenience. At that time the only known method of securing additional queens, was by means of depriving a colony of the queen. The queenless colony in its anxiety to make sure of replacing the lost mother, would usually prepare a number of cells and rear several more queens than needed. The ripe cells were taken from the hive before the emergence of the first queen, and given to nuclei or queenless colonies. As compared to present wholesale methods, this plan was crude and unsatisfactory. However, a careful beekeeper could by this means make considerable increase artificially, or provide young queens to replace undesirable ones.

In the first edition of his "Hive and the Honey-Bee," Langstroth describes his method of queen rearing by means of one queen in three hives. Two hives were deprived of their queens which were used to make artificial swarms or nuclei, at intervals of a week. When the first hive had been queenless for nine days, there were several sealed queen cells, which were counted, on the tenth day these were removed for use and a laying queen was taken from a third hive, C, and given to the first hive where she was permitted to lay a few days. In the meantime the second hive had been made queenless and had built cells. When these in turn were removed the queen which had been taken from the third hive, C, and placed in the first hive, was taken from the first hive and passed on to the second. The hive C, from which the queen had been taken, soon had cells ready to remove and she was replaced in her original home. Here she was permitted to stay for only a short time when she was started a second time around the circle. By keeping the queen in each hive for a period of a week at one time, sufficient eggs were laid to prevent the rapid depletion of the stock while providing a sufficient number of eggs and young larvae, to insure queen cells when she was again removed. By this simple plan he was able to get a large number of young queens and at the same time preserve the parent colonies. Whenever possible the queen cells were removed intact by taking out the frame on which they were formed and exchanging it for another from the colony, to which it was desired to give the cell. At times, however, he found it necessary to cut the cells from the combs, since several cells were often on the same comb.

For a number of years no better method was developed, and while numerous variations of the Langstroth plan were described in the beekeeping literature of the time, the only way known to secure additional queens was by means of making a colony queenless and trusting them to build cells in a natural manner. In an early edition of his "Manual of the Apiary," Cook recommended that the edges of the combs containing eggs or young larvae, be trimmed, or holes cut, somewhat after the manner known in later years as the Miller plan.

Quinby's Method.

Quinby practiced rearing queens by forming small nuclei of about a quart of bees and giving them small pieces of comb containing larvae not less than two, or more than three days old. A hole was cut in a brood comb sufficient to insert a piece of comb containing the larvae. This is described to be one inch deep and three inches long. No other brood was permitted in the hive. Concerning this plan he says: "I want new comb for the brood, as cells can be worked over out of that, better than from old and tough. New comb must be carefully handled. If none but old, tough comb is to be had, cut the cells down to one-fourth inch in depth. The knife must be sharp to leave it smooth and not tear it."

While practicing the method just described, he said in his book, that in many respects he preferred to rear queens in a strong colony made queenless.

The Alley Plan.

Henry Alley made a distinct advance when he developed his plan of using strips of worker comb containing eggs or just hatched larvae. Before describing his method of preparing these cells, it is best, perhaps, to outline his plan of preparing the bees to receive them so that his whole method may be clearly explained.

He recommended taking the best colony in the apiary to use as cell builders. After the queen had been found, her bees were brushed into a "swarm box," which has a wire-cloth top and bottom, to admit the air. "The bees should be kept queenless for at least ten hours in the swarming box, else the eggs given them for cell building will be destroyed. Soon after being put into it they will miss their queen and keep up an uproar until released."

The bees in the swarm box were kept in a cool room or cellar and fed a pint of syrup. In the meantime the old hive has been removed and a queen rearing hive placed on the old stand. At night the bees are returned to the new hive on the old stand and given cell building material provided as follows:

In the center of the hive containing the breeding queen an empty comb has been placed four days previously. This will now contain eggs and hatching larvae. The bees are carefully brushed off this comb and it is taken into a warm room to be cut into strips. With a thin, sharp knife, which must be kept warm to avoid bruising the comb, the comb is cut through every alternate row of cells. After the comb has been cut up into strips, these are laid flat on a table and the cells on one side of the midrib are cut down to within a quarter of an inch of the

Fig. 17.   Comb cut down for cell building, by Alley.

septum as shown in Fig. 17. Every alternate egg or larva is crushed by means of a match pressed gently into the shallow

Fig. 18.   Every alternate egg is crushed with a match twirled between the fingers.

cells and twirled between the thumb and finger, Fig. 18.   This gives room enough for a queen cell over each remaining one, Fig. 19.   A frame containing a brood comb with about one-half

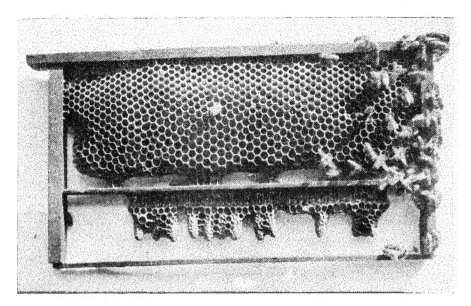

Fig. 19.   Queen-cells by the Alley plan. [From Productive Beekeeping.]

cut away is used as a foundation for the prepared strip. The uncut side of the strip is dipped into melted beeswax and at once pressed against the lower edge of the comb. It is necessary to use care to have this melted wax of just the right temperature so as not to destroy the eggs by overheating them, while at the same time warm enough to run readily and stick to the dry comb. The shallow cells, those which have been trimmed, open downward in the same position as a natural queen cell built under the swarming impulse.

The care of the cell building colonies, emerging queens, etc., is the same by this method as any other and will be found in detail further on. See page 63. Aside from the strips of prepared cells, no brood will be given to the queenless bees, and they will concentrate their attention on building cells, with the result that a considerable number of fine cells will be secured.

CHAPTER VI

Present Day Methods.

While most queen breeders of the present day use some modification of the Doolittle cell cup method, a few still cling to the Alley plan or some modification of it. J. L. Strong, a well known queen breeder of Iowa, who has but recently retired, continued to follow the Alley plan in detail until the end of his queen breeding career. Mr. Strong was a beekeeper for half a century and engaged in commercial queen rearing for about twenty-five years. The Davis queen yards in Tennessee use a modification of this method, using drone comb instead of worker comb. This necessitates grafting, as with artificial cell cups.

The Davis Method of Using Drone Comb.

At the Davis yards in Tennessee, a modification of the Alley plan is used. Instead of cutting down worker comb in which eggs have already been laid as in the Alley plan, they cut down fresh drone comb wherever available. This necessitates grafting of larvae the same as in the cell cup method later to be described. Strips of new drone comb are cut down, as already described, and fastened to wood supports. Royal jelly is taken from queen cells the same as in the cell cup method, and a small quantity placed in each drone cell which it is desired to use. Worker larvae from the hive occupied by the breeding queen are then carefully lifted from their cells by means of a toothpick or grafting tool, and placed in these prepared cells. Every third or fourth drone cell can be used in this manner. These cells are given to strong colonies to be built, the same as by the Alley plan or cell cup plan.

Fig. 20. A batch of finished cells grafted with drone comb at the Davis apiaries.

Mr. J. M. Davis has tried about all the systems so far given to the public during the nearly fifty years that he has been engaged in queen breeding. After giving the Doolittle cell cup method an extended trial, he abandoned it in favor of the plan above described. By this plan, it is possible to get large batches of fine cells, although it becomes necessary to have combs drawn above excluders and without foundation, in order to get a sufficient supply of drone comb for the thousands of cells which are built in a yard, doing an exten-

Fig. 21.   Cutting away cells built on drone comb.

sive business. Figure 20 shows one batch of 37 finished cells by this method. Cells built by this plan are not as convenient to remove and place in nursery cages or mating nuclei as those having the wood base.. These must be cut apart as in Figure 21. This also necessitates some special means of carrying them about to avoid injury to the tender occupants. For this purpose a block with 24 holes bored in it is used at the Davis apiaries. As the cells are cut from the frame they are placed in the block, in the natural position. The block is easily carried from hive to hive while placing the ripe cells. Figure 22.

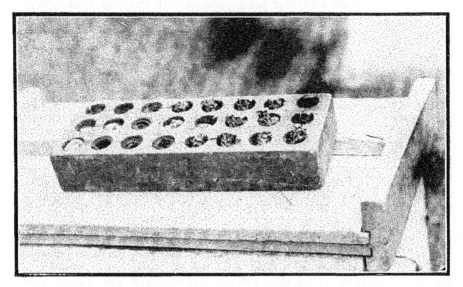

Fig. 22. The cell block enables the queen breeder to carry a batch of cells right side up without danger of injury.

Natural Built Cells by the Miller Plan.

What has, of late, been known as the Miller method of rearing queens, was probably not entirely original with him, but has been used in more or less the same form for many years. However, Dr. C. C. Miller has given the method new prominence, and brought it forcibly to public attention. In offering it, he did not even claim to be putting forth anything entirely new, but presented it as a very satisfactory method

for the honey producer to provide himself with a limited number
of queens with little trouble.   The plan was so simple that it
made an instant appeal, and has been widely published and
generally used under the name of the Miller Plan.   The author
probably can present the matter in no other way so well as to
copy Doctor Miller's original article concerning it from the
American Bee Journal, August, 1912:

> Yet it is not necessary to use artificial cells.   The plan I use for
> rearing queens for myself requires nothing of the kind.   And it gives
> as good queens as can be reared.   I do not say that it is the best plan
> for those who rear queens on a large scale to sell.   But for the honey
> producer who wishes to rear his own queens I have no hesitation in
> recommending it.   I have reared hundreds of queens by what are con-
> sidered the latest and most approved plans for queen breeders; and so
> think that I am competent to judge, and I feel sure that this simple
> plan is the best for me as a honey producer.   I will give it as briefly as
> possible.
>
> Into an empty brood frame, at a distance of two or three inches
> from each end, fasten a starter of foundation about two inches wide
> at the top, and coming down to a point within an inch or two of the bot-
> tom bar.   Put it in the hive containing your best queen.   To avoid
> having it filled with drone-comb, take out of the hive, either for a few
> days or permanently, all but two frames of brood, and put your empty
> frame between these two.   In a week or so you will find this frame
> half filled with beautiful virgin comb, such as bees delight to use for
> queen-cells.   It will contain young brood with an outer margin of eggs.
> Trim away with a sharp knife all the outer margin of comb which con-
> tains eggs, except, perhaps, a very few eggs next to the youngest brood.
> This you will see is very simple.   Any beekeeper can do it the first time
> trying, and it is all that is necessary to take the place of preparing arti-
> ficial cells.
>
> Now put this "queen cell stuff," if I may thus call the prepared
> frame, into the middle of a very strong colony from which the queen
> has been removed.   The bees will do the rest, and you will have as
> good cells as you can possibly have with any kind of artificial cells.
> You may think that the bees will start "wild cells" on their own comb.
> They won't; at least they never do to amount to anything, and, of course,
> you needn't use those.   The soft, new comb with abundant room at
> the edge, for cells, is so much more to their taste that it has a practical
> monopoly of all cells started.   In about ten days the sealed cells are
> ready to be cut out and used wherever desired.

This plan is especially useful to the novice or to the beekeeper wishing for but a few queens at one time.   It is simple,
easy and never failing under any normal conditions.

Our illustration, Figure 23, shows this method with four
strips of foundation used to start, instead of two as Doctor
Miller suggests in his article.

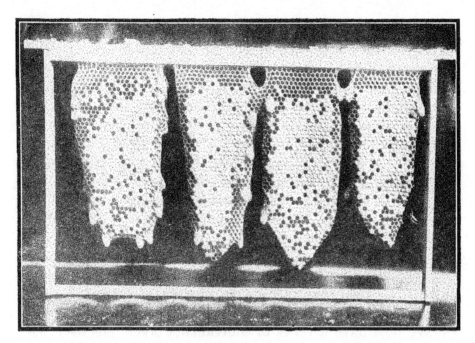

Fig. 23.   Queen-cells built naturally by the Miller plan.

Big Batches of Natural Cells by the Hopkins or Case Method.

Many extensive honey producers who desire to make short work of requeening an entire apiary, and who do not care to bother with mating boxes or other extra paraphernalia, make use of the Case method, which has been somewhat modified from its original form.   This method is advocated by such well known beekeepers as Oscar Dines of New York and Henry Brenner of Texas.   The plan was first used in Europe

To begin with, a strong colony is made queenless to serve as a cell building colony.   Then a frame of brood is removed from the center of the brood nest of the colony containing the breeding queen from whose progeny it is desired to rear the queens.   In its place is given a tender new comb not previously used for brood rearing.   At the end of four days this should be well filled with eggs and just hatching larvae.   If the queen does not make use of this new comb at once, it should not be removed until four days from the time when she begins to lay in its cells. At that time nearly all the cells should be filled with eggs and some newly hatched larvae.

This new comb freshly filled is ideal for cell building purposes. The best side of the comb is used for the queen cells and is prepared by destroying two rows of worker cells and leaving one, beginnning at the top of the frame. This is continued clear across the comb. We will now have rows of cells running lengthwise of the comb, but if used without further preparation the queen cells will be built in bunches, that it will be impossible to separate without injury to many of them. Accordingly we begin at one end, and destroy two cells and leave one in each row, cutting them down to the midrib but being careful not to cut through and spoil the opposite side. Some practice destroying three or four rows of cells, and leaving one to give more room between the finished queen cells.

We now have a series of individual worker cells over the entire surface of the comb, with a half inch or more of space between them. The practice varies somewhat with different beekeepers beyond this point. However, this prepared surface is laid flatwise with cells facing down, over the brood nest of the queenless colony, first taking care to make sure that any queen cells they may have started are destroyed. In general, it is recommended that the colony be queenless about seven days before giving this comb. By this time there will be no larvae left in the hive young enough for rearing queens, and the bees will be very anxious to restore normal conditions. Some beekeepers simply take away all unsealed brood, rather than leave the bees queenless so long.

As generally used, this method requires a special box or frame to hold the prepared comb. This is closed on one side to prevent the escape of heat upward and to hold the comb securely in place. Figure 24. Some kind of support is necessary to hold the comb far enough above the frames to leave plenty of room for drawing large queen cells. It is also advisable to cover the comb with a cloth which can be tucked snugly

Fig. 24. Frame for holding comb horizontally above brood-nest for getting queen-cells by the Case method.

around it, to hold the heat of the cluster. By using an empty comb-honey super above the cluster, there is room enough for the prepared comb and also for plenty of cloth to make all snug and warm.

Strong colonies only should be used for this, as for any other method of queen rearing. If all conditions are favorable, the beekeeper will secure a maximum number of cells. From seventy-five to one hundred fine cells are not unusual. By killing the old queens a day or two before the ripe cells are given it is possible to requeen a whole apiary by this method with a minimum of labor. According to Miss Emma Wilson, it is possible to get very good results by this method, without mutilating the comb, although it is probable that a smaller number of queen cells will be secured. By laying the comb on its side as practiced in this connection, the cells can be removed with a very slight effort and with a minimum of danger.

The Doolittle Cell Cup Method.

Nine queen breeders in every ten, it is safe to say, use the Doolittle cell cups.   While it is possible to rear queens on a commercial scale by other methods, few queen breeders care to do so.   One can control conditions so nicely by the use of artificial wax cups and can determine so nearly how many cells will be finished at a given time, that this method is in all but universal use in commercial queen breeding apiaries.   Most of the extensive queen breeders count on turning out queens at a uniform rate, increasing the number as the season advances to keep pace with the probable demand.   It is of no advantage to a breeder to produce five hundred ripe cells at a time when he has market for only a dozen queens.   He estimates as nearly as possible the demand for the season and establishes a sufficient number of mating nuclei to care for the queens as they emerge.   During the height of the season a queen is only permitted to lay enough eggs to enable the breeder to satisfy himself that she is fertile and otherwise normal.   Queens thus follow each other in rapid succession in the various mating boxes, throughout the season.

It was the difficulty of keeping up a dependable supply of queens to supply his increasing trade that led G. M. Doolittle of New York state to experiment with artificial cells.   The successful outcome of his extended experiments has largely revolutionized the queen trade.   They have already been in use for about thirty years.   One can make from one hundred and fifty to two hundred of these wax cups per hour, so perhaps this plan can be followed as easily as any from the point of time required in the various operations.   Dealers in bee supplies now list these artificial cells for sale at a small price, and many buy them already prepared.   They can be used either with or without a wood cell base.   When used without the base they are attached to wood strips by means of melted beeswax.   However, the wood base is very generally used, since the cells can be changed about with much less danger of injury.   A sharp pointed tack is imbedded in the base, which makes it very easy to attach them to frame supports on which they are inserted into the hives. Figure 25 shows a frame of newly prepared cells ready for the hive. It will be seen that a strip of foundation is used above the wood supporting the cell cups. This will soon be drawn by the bees and filled with honey. More often the beekeeper cuts away part of a comb already drawn for use in this way.

Mr. Doolittle used a wood rake tooth as a form on which to mold the cells. Lacking this, a round stick about the size of a lead pencil, but with carefully rounded end, may be used. Beeswax is melted in a small dish over a lamp or on a stove of moderate heat. It must not be kept too hot, otherwise it does not cool rapidly enough. A mark should be made on the stick nine-sixteenths of an inch from the end, and the stick dipped into water to prevent the wax from sticking. After giving it a quick jerk to throw off the water it is then dipped into the melted wax up to the mark. The dipping is done quickly, twirling the stick around as it is lifted out to distribute the wax evenly. As soon as the wax is sufficiently hardened, it is dipped again, this time not quite so deep. The form is thus

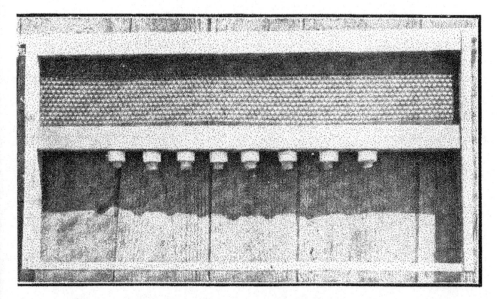

Fig. 25. Frame of prepared cups by the Doolittle method.

dipped again and again, each time lacking about a thirty-second of an inch of going as deep as before, until the base of the cell is sufficiently thick to make a good cell.

These artificial cells answer the purpose as well as those built by the bees, and if other conditions are normal the bees accept them readily. If wood blocks are used they are now ready to be attached to the blocks, or if not, direct to the wood strips. Figure 25.

For use, it becomes necessary to supply each cell cup with a small amount of royal jelly, and then with a toothpick or grafting tool carefully lift larva, not to exceed thirty-six hours old, from a worker cell and place it on the jelly in the prepared artificial cell.

CHAPTER VII

Preparation for Cells.

Whether one uses the Alley plan or some of its modifications, or the Doolittle cell cup method, certain stages of the process of getting the cells built may be the same. A supply of royal jelly will be necessary to begin with only where grafting, or changing the larvae from worker cells into prepared cells, is practiced. The preparation of colonies for building cells, finishing them and caring for them until ready for emergence of the young queens, is very similar by any of these methods.

There are numerous variations of the treatment of colonies in preparation for cell building, and several of these will be described in an effort to treat the whole subject in a comprehensive manner.

Getting Jelly to Start With.

If the beekeeper wishes to start cells early in the season before there has been any preparation for swarming, it is sometimes difficult to secure a supply of royal jelly readily; especially is this true when the colonies are still weak from wintering. The first thing to do is to look carefully for supersedure cells, when making the spring examination of the apiary. Failing queens may be replaced at any season, and one or two cells will be built in anticipation of the supersedure. If a cell is found, this difficulty is at once disposed of, providing it is at the proper stage. The royal jelly is found in the bottom of the queen cells and is a thick white paste, very similar in appearance to the paste ordinarily used for library purposes or mounting photographs. Sometimes, when it is quite thick, it is desirable to thin it slightly by the addition of a small quantity of saliva or a drop of warm water. Only a minute amount of

jelly is placed in each of the prepared cups, so that a well supplied queen cell will provide a sufficient quantity to supply
thirty to fifty of them.

If no cells containing jelly are found, the usual plan is to
remove the queen from a vigorous colony and permit them to
start cells. The author very much dislikes to remove queens
except when absolutely necessary, and prefers some other
plan. A simple way is to place a wire cloth over the top of a
strong colony in place of the cover. On this set a hive body
containing at least three frames of brood in the various stages,
being sure that there is no queen on the frames, and that there
is plenty of newly hatched larvae. All adhering bees should be
left on the combs. The cover is then placed over all and the
hive left closed for two days, when there will be an abundant
supply of royal jelly available.

The Author's Plan.

The author, not being engaged in queen rearing commer-
cially, can choose a favorable time for rearing such queens as
are necessary to make increase or for requeening. While the
method seldom fails even under unfavorable conditions with
him, it is very possible that it might not be satisfactory under
some conditions.

To begin with, the queen is found and placed, on the comb
on which she is, in an empty hivebody. Sometimes the remainder of the space is filled with empty drawn combs, sometimes
one or more frames of brood are added, as circumstances dic-
tate. The hivebody containing the queen is then placed on
the hivestand in the position where the colony had already been
placed. Above the hivebody containing the queen is placed a
queen excluder, to prevent the queen from going above. If
the weather is warm so that there is no longer any danger
of chilling brood from dividing the cluster into two parts, an
empty set of extracting combs is placed over the excluder.
The original hive containing most of the brood is now placed
on top of this empty chamber. Twenty-four hours later the

bees are given a frame of cellcups containing larvae. These cups are placed in the hive in the same manner as usual, except that they have no royal jelly. A thin syrup made with sugar and water or honey thinned with water is then poured freely over the tops of these frames. The worker bees gorge themselves freely with the syrup and, since the brood in the upper chamber is so far from the queen below, the bees are easily stimulated to start queen cells. Usually from one to three of these dry cells will be accepted, and two days later will furnish an abundant supply of royal jelly for grafting purposes. A second lot of cells is now prepared with jelly, and these are given to the bees in the upper story in the same manner. Syrup is poured over the frames as freely as before, with the result that a large portion of the cells are likely to be accepted. The author does not claim that the idea is altogether original with him, but simply outlines it as his method of practice. Feeding the bees freely at the time of giving a batch of cells is rather common practice among the queen breeders in certain localities. By this method, it is easily possible to secure a supply of royal jelly without dequeening a colony or interfering with the laying of the queen. If it is too cold to place an empty super between the brood nest and the brood in the upper story, the plan will usually work with only the excluder between. After the weather becomes warm enough, it is easily possible to continue building cells indefinitely above the same colony, by lifting the brood above as fast as sealed in the brood nest. The young bees emerging in the upper chamber continue to supply nurses as needed. It will be readily apparent that to be successful this plan requires a strong colony

Transferring the Larvae.

Some beekeepers make a practice of placing a frame of cellcups in the hive over night in advance of the grafting. The idea is that the bees will work them over, smooth and polish them, thus placing them in more attractive condition for the acceptance of the prepared cells. The author has never been

able to convince himself that this plan brings enough better
results, in practice, to justify the extra trouble, where large
numbers of queens are to be reared.

The cellcups are placed in the wood bases and fastened in
place as shown in Figure 25. Commercial queen breeders
usually have two or three bars of cells in each frame instead of
only one. About fifteen cellcups to each bar is not unusual,
so that with a liberal number accepted it is often possible to
get from thirty to forty finished cells in each batch. Figure 26.

At this stage the grafting house described on page 31 is
very desirable. The queen cells from which the royal jelly
is to be taken, together with the prepared cellcups and a frame
of newly hatching brood from the breeding colony are now taken
to the grafting house or into a warm room for the final preparation. For transferring the jelly and the larvae, there are spe-
cially prepared tools in the market. These look very much like
knitting needles with one end flattened and slightly bent to
one side. However, one can do very well with a quill cut down
to a strip about a sixteenth of an inch in width, with the end
bent in similar manner. Even a toothpick can be made to
serve quite well.

An ingenious device for transferring larvae is described by
John Grubb of Woodmont, Pa He uses a small stick of wood
about three-sixteenths of an inch thick and four inches long,
one end of which is whittled down to a long tapering point.
A long horsehair is doubled, then twisted together, and doubled
again. Both ends are laid on the stick, the circular center
extending beyond the end. Fine thread is wrapped around the
hair and the stick, to hold all firmly. The doubled hair makes
a circle about a tenth of an inch in diameter beyond the pointed
end of the stick. With this horsehair spoon it is an easy matter to lift a larva from a cell and transfer it to a cellcup. It
is easily and quickly made and materials necessary are usually
within easy reach.

First a bit of royal jelly is placed in each cellcup, and then
a larva about twenty-four to thirty-six hours old is carefully
lifted from its cell and placed on the jelly. There is some

Fig. 26. A batch of cells by the cell-cup method.

difference of opinion as to the proper age of larvae, but all agree that larvae more than three days old should never be used. Nobody holds that better queens can be reared from larvae two days old than from younger larvae, although some think that as good results can be obtained. The majority seem to favor larvae from twelve to twenty-four hours old, with some

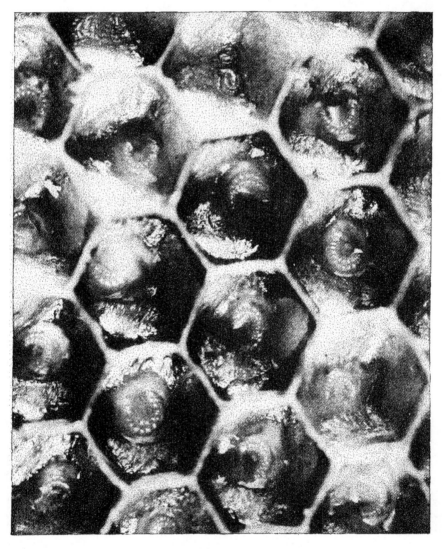

Fig. 27. Larvae not to exceed thirty-six hours old should be used for grafting.

strong advocates of thirty-six hours as the proper age. Figure 27. However, it may safely be said that twenty-four to thirty-six hours is as old as larvae should be for this purpose. Probably up to this age as good or better results will be obtained as from the use of younger ones.

Something has already been said about the importance of selecting the breeding stock carefully. This is a vital matter if good results are to come from the breeder's work. The larvae used in grafting should be the product of the best queen available.

At Figure 27 we show the magnified larvae in the cells at about the proper age for grafting. Sladen recommends that larvae not quite as large as a lettuce seed be used. With a little experience one will soon come to tell readily the approximate age of the larvae by the appearance.

CHAPTER VIII

Getting Cells Started.

Fig. 28. Only strong colonies should be used for building or finishing cells.

For building cells one must have strong colonies, Figure 28, and to insure this condition, one must have his bees in good shape in early spring. While it is often advocated that stimulative feeding be resorted to early, in order to build the colonies up to a sufficient strength, the author inclines to the belief that colonies in two stories will build up just as rapidly if there is an abundance of sealed honey in the hive, as is possible with stimulative feeding. Sometimes it seems that uncapping a portion of the honey has a stimulating effect, but feeding in small quantities, for the purpose of stimulating the bees to greater activity, rarely seems necessary until the time comes to give them the cells. At this time feeding is often needed in order to get large batches accepted and finished. When honey is coming in from natural sources, feeding is, of course, unnecessary.

The real problem is to get the bees into the right temper to accept the cells readily, and finish a large portion of them properly. This point has been touched upon rather indirectly, already, under the discussion of the various methods. A strong colony which is preparing to supersede the queen is very desirable at this time. Such a colony will accept cells readily and will supply them with royal jelly abundantly. No better cells can be had than those built in a supersedure colony. It will pay to look through the apiary very carefully in search of such a colony, rather than to resort to artificial conditions. A colony which is preparing to swarm, will do very well, also, only they must be watched carefully, to make sure that a swarm does not issue as soon as the cells are sealed. When a colony is found to have queen cells already built which contain eggs or larvae, these cells may be destroyed and a frame of prepared cells given. Little attention need be paid to the presence of the queen, for she will not disturb the new cells under such conditions.

If no colony is to be had which is already in the cell-building notion, it then becomes necessary to stimulate the cell-building instinct artificially. There are several methods of doing this.

Removing Queen and Brood.

Probably the most generally practiced method is to take a strong colony, and remove the queen and all unsealed brood. Empty combs and those which contain only honey and pollen are left in the hive. The queen should be placed in a nucleus, or given to another colony where needed. All bees should be carefully brushed from the combs containing the brood in order to leave as large a force of nurse bees as possible. The brood is then given to another colony to be cared for.

About ten or twelve hours later the bees will be in the mood to build queen cells. Being without brood, the nurse bees will be abundantly supplied with food for the larvae, and will accept a batch of prepared cells very eagerly.

When giving the cells, it is well to follow the practice of some of the most extensive breeders and feed liberally at the moment, to insure a larger portion of cells accepted. For this purpose an ordinary garden sprinkler serves very well. Thin sugar syrup is sprinkled freely over the tops of the frames as described previously. The bees gorge themselves in cleaning up the syrup and anxiously seek larvae to be fed. This method of feeding is desirable at the time of giving cells by any method.

Some breeders leave the prepared cells in the colony to which they are first given until they are sealed. However, a larger number of first class cells will usually be secured by working two colonies together, one as a cell-building colony and the second as a cell-finishing colony. The cell-finishing colony should be equally strong with the cell-starting colony, but not all the brood is taken from it. At the time that the brood is taken from the first colony, part of the brood is removed from another, and the remainder raised above an excluder, leaving the queen in the brood nest below on one frame of brood, and with empty combs in which to continue laying. This we will call the finishing colony.

Twenty-four hours after the prepared cells have been given to the queenless and broodless bees in the cell-starting hive, we will probably find most of the cells partly built, and the larvae abundantly supplied with royal jelly. If we leave them as they are, some of these cells are likely to be neglected, so that not all will come to maturity. We may now safely remove these cells and after carefully brushing off the nurse bees with a feather, give them to the cell-finishing colony, placing the frames above the excluder. By this time the bees in the second colony will have been forty-eight hours separated from the queen which still remains below the excluder. Since no eggs have been laid with the brood above for this period, the bees are in much the same condition as a colony with a failing queen and accordingly accept the cells as readily, as a rule, as a supersedure colony will do.

When the batch of started cells is taken from the starting colony, it is given a second lot of newly prepared cells. This may be repeated regularly for some time. However, the same bees cannot serve as nurses for very long and it will be necessary

Fig. 29.   A strong cell-finishing colony.

to supply the starting colony with frames of sealed brood ready to emerge at frequent intervals if the same colony is used as a cell-starting colony for more than ten days. Usually the number of cells accepted in each batch will soon begin to diminish, so that it will be desirable to prepare another colony for this purpose after eight or ten days.

There is a great difference in individual colonies as to the number of cells built, and it sometimes becomes necessary to experiment a bit to find the best colonies for this purpose. Some colonies will build double the number of cells that others will build. An extensive breeder will find it necessary to have several cell-building colonies at one time. Figure 29 shows a strong cell-finishing colony at the Davis apiary in Tennessee.

The Swarm Box.

Alley used much the same plan as above described, except that he first found the queen and then shook all the bees into a swarm box which is made by placing a wirecloth bottom and cover on an ordinary box of suitable size. The bees were smoked before shaking them into the box to induce them to gorge themselves with honey, and then they were confined in the box from morning until evening. The wirecloth admits plenty of air and by the time the bees are placed in a hive for cell building, they will recognize their hopelessly queenless condition, and be ready to accept the prepared cells with little delay.   Alley gave eggs in strips of natural comb, instead of the prepared cells, it will be remembered, but the principle is the same.   He left the bees queenless in the swarm box for at least ten hours.   He also fed the bees syrup while confined in the box.

Rearing Queens in Queenright Colonies.

The author prefers to rear queens in a queenright colony, since it is not so difficult to maintain normal conditions over a long period of time, and the bees are not so sensitive to fluctuations in weather conditions or honeyflow.   It is not always possible to make a success with the first batch of cells given by this plan, but once accepted the same colony can be kept busy rearing cells for weeks, or even all summer if desired.

One plan which is followed by successful breeders is to select a strong colony for cell building.   Remove the cover, and put a queen excluder in its place.   Then take enough frames of brood from several different colonies to fill a second brood-chamber above the excluder, leaving one vacant space. Care must be used to make sure that no queen is on the frames placed in the second story.   The vacant space is left as near the center of the colony as possible, and a few hours later a frame of prepared cells is placed there, feeding the bees with syrup from the sprinkling can at the time the cells are given. If this first batch of cells is not readily accepted try again the following day.   After four days a second batch can be given, and a new batch every four days thereafter.   By this plan the cells are left with the colony until ready to be given to the nuclei.   It only becomes necessary to add two or three frames of sealed brood every week to provide the colony with plenty of young bees for nurses, to continue cell building indefinitely. About ten to fifteen sealed cells can be secured from a single colony every four days by this plan.   If a heavy honeyflow comes on, it may become necessary to add supers between the brood nest below and the cell-building chamber above, since the old queen continues to lay in normal manner below the excluder. By this method the cell-building colony will give a crop of honey as well as queens. The addition of so much brood from other colonies will keep the cell-building colony very strong throughout the season. Of course, frames of honey must be removed from time to time as frames of brood are given, and, during a good flow, it may become necessary to remove frames of honey quite often to prevent crowding in the cell-building chamber.

Feeding.

During a dearth of nectar it often becomes necessary to resort to stimulative feeding to induce the bees to continue cell building by any of these methods. Of course, a queenless colony will build some cells under almost any conditions, but to get good cells in sufficient numbers, a fresh supply of food must continue coming to the hive daily. If there is none in the field a pint or more of thin syrup should be fed daily, preferably at night, to prevent robbing.

CHAPTER IX

Care of Finished Cells.

About four days after the prepared cell cups are given to the bees, the finished cells will be sealed, Figure 30. If the weather is warm they may be placed in cages and transferred to other colonies for safe keeping, until time for the young queens to emerge. However, in cool weather, there is danger that the young queens will be chilled and injured, if the cells are placed in cages so that the nurses can no longer warm them by direct contact. Most breeders leave the cells to the care of the bees until the evening of the ninth day. The cells are then caged or given directly to the nuclei, where they are to be

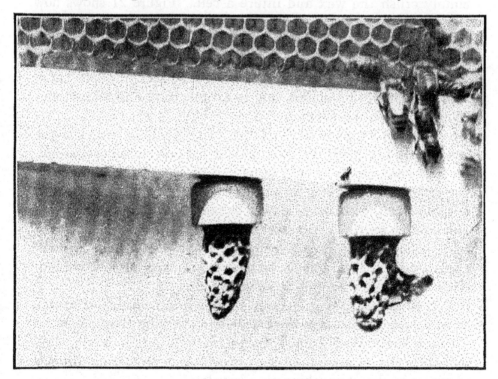

Fig. 30. Finished cells by the Doolittle method.

mated.   In general, it is better to place the cell at once in
the nucleus.

Great care must always be used in handling sealed queen
cells.   Any slight jar is likely to dislodge the nymph from its bed
of royal jelly and injure it seriously.   The bees which may cluster
about the cells may be driven off by smoking them or by carefully brushing them away.   The longer the cells are left undisturbed, the less the danger of injury to the young queens.   The
bees should never be shaken from a frame containing queen
cells.

It is necessary to separate cells built by the Alley plan by
cutting with a sharp knife.   The knife should be kept warm
to get best results.   Otherwise, instead of cutting freely it may
simply crush the wax and injure a cell.   Figure 21 shows how
the cells may be cut apart.

It is important, also, to keep the cells right side up at all
times.   Some breeders use a cell block such as may be seen at
Figure 22.   This enables the breeder to carry a whole batch
to the apiary to be placed, one at a time, in the nuclei, without
danger of injuring them.

It often happens that a batch of cells will be ripe and the
nuclei not yet ready to receive them for one reason or another.
In that case, candy should be placed in the nursery cages, and
the cells placed in them on the ninth or tenth day after the cells
are given to the bees.   It should be remembered that the queens
will emerge on the fifteenth or sixteenth day after the eggs were
laid.   Should a virgin queen emerge before the cells are removed
and cared for, she is likely to destroy at once all that remain.
Thus all the beekeeper's labor is for naught.

It is necessary to exercise some care in extremely hot weather to avoid overheating the cells when carrying them about in
the hot sun.   Well known queen breeders admit having lost
valuable cells on more than one occasion by overheating through
exposure to direct sunshine on a hot day.

In placing the cells in the nuclei the cell should be gently
pushed into the side of a comb just above the brood, if there is
brood.   However, it often happens that no brood is present

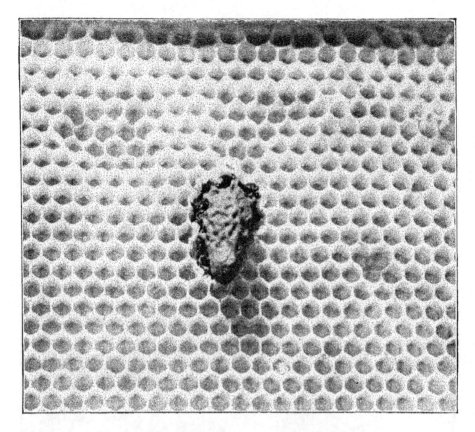

Fig. 31.   Placing cell in nucleus without brood.

in a nucleus when a cell is placed.   In that event it should be
set into the comb near the center of the hive.   Figure 31.

Use of Cell Protectors.

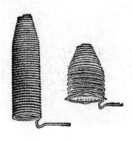

Fig. 32.
Cell protectors.

If a nucleus has been queenless for
twelve hours when a ripe cell is introduced,
there will seldom be any need for using
protectors.   However, it often happens
that the breeder will have ripe cells ready
which he wishes to place as fast as the
queens are removed.   When the bees
destroy queen cells they do so by opening
the cell at the side, and never from the

end. Taking advantage of this fact a wire protector has been made which remains open at the end, thus permitting the queen to emerge without further attention, Figure 32. By the time the queen is ready to emerge, the bees will discover the absence of the old queen and the newcomer will be welcomed.

Formation of Nuclei.

In the chapter on equipment for queen rearing, the various styles of mating boxes and hives have been described. If the standard hive is used, the formation of nuclei is a simple matter. As many colonies as may be needed to make the desired number of nuclei are broken up, and the combs together with adhering bees are placed in the nuclei. One frame with the old queen is left in the old hive, and it is usually well to leave a second frame of brood with her, to enable her to build

Fig. 33. A queen-mating yard composed of standard hives, each divided into two parts.

up the colony again more rapidly. The rest of the space is filled with empty combs. One frame of brood and bees, together with one empty comb or one containing honey, is placed in each nucleus, Figure 33. The entrance is then stopped with grass to prevent the escape of the bees for several hours. By the time they have gnawed their way out they will become accustomed to the new condition, and most of them will remain in the new position. Unless the frame given is well supplied with brood, it is desirable to give two frames to each nucleus.

A day or two later sealed queen cells may be given safely. As the season advances, the demand for queens increases, and the breeder will find it necessary to increase the number of mating nuclei. As each queen is allowed to lay for a short time in the nucleus before caged for shipment, many of the nuclei will build up rapidly. From time to time one will be found which can spare a frame of brood and bees as already described. At the close of the season these nuclei are united to make them strong enough to winter as full colonies.

Stocking Mating Boxes or Baby Nuclei.

Much difficulty is sometimes experienced in getting the bees to stay in these small hives. The plan usually recommended is to shake the bees into a wirecloth cage and confine them there for several hours. Four or five hours later run in a virgin queen among them. At nightfall, shake them into the mating box and leave them undisturbed for a few days. Some of the old bees may return to their former hive the next morning, but most of them are likely to remain. There is some danger that they may swarm out with the queen when she comes out for her mating flight. However, after one queen has been successfully mated and there is some brood in the little hive, there will be less trouble with the next one. These little hives must be watched to make sure that they do not at any time become short of food, otherwise they sometimes swarm out and leave the brood.

The available space is so small that the queen can be left

but a very short time. The two little combs are soon filled with eggs and with no more room to lay, the queen may lead a small swarm, and thus desert the hive.

Another plan of stocking these hives is to shake a lot of bees from several hives into a box with wirecloth top and bottom similar to the Alley swarm box, and keep them confined for several hours. It is desirable that these bees be brought from a distance, if possible. When ready to stock the mating hives, wet the bees enough to prevent flying readily and dip them out with a tin dipper, turning a sufficient quantity into each compartment. A supply of virgin queens is ready at hand, and as each compartment is filled, a virgin is dropped into a dish of honey and then into the compartment with the bees. The entrance is opened at night to prevent the loss of bees before the excitement subsides. This is the plan practiced at the Root yards.

CHAPTER X

Combining Mating with Making of Increase.

The usual methods of artificial increase, such as division or formation of nuclei to be built up, weaken the colony to a considerable extent. Should the season prove unfavorable

Fig. 34.   A queen-rearing apiary in Tennessee.

after nuclei are formed, it may be necessary to feed them for a long period of time, only in the end to find it necessary to unite them again to get them strong enough for winter. Getting queens mated in an upper story is not new; yet there are some elements in the following plan which differ somewhat from methods previously given to the public.

The author has experimented to a limited extent in the hope of finding a plan which takes nothing from the parent colony, other than the honey necessary to rear the brood composing the new colony. There is no risk, since the old colony is not weakened by removing part of the field force, and the division is not made until the new colony is strong enough to shift for itself under almost any conditions. The following plan comes near realizing this ideal, having been uniformly successful in a limited way, even under unfavorable conditions. This is the outgrowth of a system of swarm control in the pro-

Fig. 35.   Queen-mating nuclei under the pine trees of Alabama.

duction of extracted honey, as described in Productive Beekeeping.

If the extracted honey producer can keep his colony together during the season. he should be able to get maximum results. Some increase is necessary in most any apiary, with any kind of system, to replace such colonies as are lost through failing queens, poor wintering or other causes, even though the beekeeper does not care to make extensions.

If the bees can be kept from swarming and the young queen be mated in a separate compartment, she can rear her own colony in due time, and they can be removed without reducing the product of the old queen, whose progeny will remain with the parent colony.

To begin with, when the colony becomes populous, place the queen on a frame of brood in an empty hivebody and fill out with empty combs. This is set on the regular hivestand occupied by the colony. The working force coming from the field will find their queen with an abundance of room in which to lay. This is the system of swarm control advocated by Demaree to this point. Now place a queen excluder over the hivebody containing the queen, and over this, a super of empty combs. On top of these is set the original hivebody containing the brood. A hole is bored in this upper hivebody to give the bees an extra entrance above. About twenty-four hours later a ripe queen cell is placed in the upper story with the brood. The queen will emerge in a day or two, and, in due time, will leave the hive on her mating flight, by way of the augur hole. Within a few days more she will be laying in the upper hivebody, while the activities of the bees will continue without interruption in the lower story. Within three weeks all the brood from the old queen (in the upper story) will have emerged. The brood which now appears in the upper story is a net addition to the resources of the colony, and, when the upper story is nearly filled with brood, it can be removed and placed on a new stand without checking the work of the colony.

To illustrate: A strong colony was given a queen cell as above described on May 21st. On July 14th, the upper hivebody with a young queen and seven frames of brood were removed to form a new colony. The strength of the parent colony was little affected apparently. Possible swarming had been prevented, temporarily at least, by the Demaree plan of placing the old queen in the empty hive below. There were two colonies better than any parent colony and swarm we had that season. In this way there had been no risk or loss. The new colony was not removed from its parent until both were provided for, neither was the possible crop cut short by dividing the working force of the parent colony at a critical time.

After three years of success with this method the author feels confident that it will prove successful on a large scale. Both queens can be left in the hive until the close of the honey-flow if desired, but there is little to be gained by leaving the queen above after her chamber is filled with brood. If both are left in the hive until late in the fall, one of the queens is likely to disappear.

If desired, the process can be repeated as soon as the upper story has been removed, as by this time the old queen will have filled the lower story with brood again. By beginning early, it should be possible to make two and possibly three new colonies, without reducing the honey crop from the parent colony to a serious extent.

This same plan might be used for the purpose of mating additional queens while making some increase, by the breeder who wishes to accomplish both ends at the same time. The method is particularly valuable to the honey producer who wishes to make some increase or rear queens for use in his own apiary, without reducing the honey crop. If increase is not especially desired, the same plan can be worked for the purpose of superseding queens. When the young queen has become nicely established in the upper chamber, the old queen can be removed from below and the position of the bodies reversed. It would be well to permit both queens to continue laying until the height of the honeyflow, in order to get as large a field force as possible for storing the crop.

CHAPTER XI

Shipping Queens.

The Benton cage, Figure 36, is almost universally used in this country for shipping purposes. So generally is it used,

Fig. 36.
The Benton mailing cage.

that it is as staple as any other item of beekeeping equipment, and can be purchased through any dealer in supplies. While cages ready stocked with candy are offered for sale, most queen breeders prefer to make their own candy and thus save some cost, as well as making it fresh as needed.

Making the Candy.

Candy for queen cages is made of honey and sugar. Under the postal regulations it is necessary to boil the honey for at least thirty minutes, unless the apiary from which it and the queens are taken has been inspected by some duly qualified officer, who is authorized to issue a certificate of health.

Care must be used, also, to make sure that the sugar used contains no starch. Powdered sugar is used for candy making, and some powdered sugar contains starch, which is detrimental to the bees confined for long in the cages.

Heat the honey and stir in as much of the powdered sugar as can be mixed in by stirring. When no more can be added by stirring, spread the powdered sugar on a mixing board and remove the dough to the board and mix it like a batch of biscuits. Some experience is necessary to determine when it is just the right consistency, neither too hard nor too soft.

According to Root, boiled honey as required by the postal regulations, does not give satisfactory results where queens are confined for long journeys. Since the idea of the regulation is to prevent the spread of disease through the honey, he recommends the use of invert sugar as a substitute for the honey.

Another kind of candy made without the use of honey, is used by some breeders. This is made by using 12 pounds of granulated sugar, 1½ pounds candy-makers' glucose, 1¼ quarts of water and ⅓ teaspoonful of cream of tartar. The cream of tartar and glucose are added to the water and heated together in a kettle. The sugar is added after the mixture comes to a boil, stirring continually while putting in the sugar. After the sugar has all been dissolved, stop stirring and let it heat to 238 degrees. Then remove from the fire and let cool to 120 degrees, and stir again until it looks like paste, when it is ready for use.

Caging the Queens.

With a few trials, one will shortly get the knack of catching a queen off the comb by her wings. Holding the cage open end downward in one hand, it is easy to so place her head in the opening that she will catch her front feet on the wood, and readily climb up into the cage. When she goes in, the thumb should be placed over the opening until a worker is caught, and ready to follow in similar manner. The novice at queen rearing often makes the mistake of placing too few bees in the cage with a queen. It is well to place as many workers in the cage as there is room for, *without crowding*, especially if the journey to be taken is a long one. As a rule the queen will be the last to die, if the bees are in normal condition when placed in the cage. It often happens that queens received from a distant place are still alive, with all their attendant workers dead in the cage. Of course the queen would not much longer survive after the workers were all dead. If the candy is properly made and sufficient in quantity, a queen will often live for several weeks in a cage, with sufficient attendants.

After queens are caged they should be placed in the mails as quickly as possible to avoid confining them longer than is necessary. Although they live for a considerable time in the cages, one can hardly believe that the confinement is conducive to the health of the queen, and the shorter the time necessary to get her to her destination, the better.

What the Buyer has a Right to Expect.

When a man sends his money for a queen in response to an advertisement, he has a right to expect that no inferior queens be sent, even though he buy untested stock. Some breeders have the reputation of sending out mismated queens that have been laying for a period long enough to show the fact, as untested queens. While few breeders guarantee that untested queens will be purely mated, to knowingly send out mismated stock, to fill orders for untested queens, is certainly dishonest. It is needless to say that no reputable breeder would do so. The breeder who expects to establish a paying business has no asset so valuable as the confidence of his customers, and this is only secured by sending out good stock and standing ready to be more than reasonable in making good any losses.

The buyer has reason to expect that he will receive pure queens, carefully reared; that the breeder shall maintain his mating nuclei in localities as free as possible from impure stock, and entirely free from disease.

Grading.

There is a great difference in the practice of different breeders in the way queens are graded. Some advertise only three grades, untested, tested and select tested queens. Others make five or more grades, adding select-untested queens and breeders. There should be some effort made to establish a standard by which a buyer can tell in advance what he is likely to get from an order for any one of these grades.

In general, an untested queen is one which has been mated and has been permitted to lay for a few days, but not long enough for the emergence of the workers. Breeders who make it a rule to send out all queens which are reared, regardless of quality, are not likely to build up a permanent business.

No poor queens should be sent out in any case, except by special understanding, and then not for breeding purposes.   There is a small demand for queens for scientific purposes, which can be supplied with mismated or otherwise inferior stock without injury to anyone.   Such queens should never be sent to a bee-keeper for introduction into normal colonies for honey production.

A tested queen is generally one which has been permitted to lay until her workers begin to emerge, and thus by their markings demonstrate the pure mating of their mother.   She should properly demonstrate other qualities also.   Select-tested and extra select-tested or choice select-tested queens are, of course, queens which for one reason or another are more promising than the average of tested queens.   Too many grades offers a good chance for the breeder to get an extra price from a buyer, without giving an equivalent in value.   It is very true that queens showing unusual traits are worth more than the gen eral run of queens, but it is difficult to grade the different degrees of behaviour into a half dozen different classes and always give a uniform value.

Virgin queens, are of course, unmated queens.   While there may be occasionally a good reason for the purchase of virgins, as a rule the practice is not to be encouraged.   The difficulty of introducing a virgin after she is several days old and consequent danger of loss, is one good reason why they should not be shipped.   The danger that they will become too old for mating before a favorable opportunity is offered, is another.   The breeder who confines his business principally to the sale of untested queens, and who gives good value for the price asked, is the one who has the fewest complaints.

Much dissatisfaction arises from the sale of breeding queens at high prices.   The buyer who pays five or ten dollars for a breeding queen, will too often expect too much of her, and, consequently, be disappointed.   Then it often happens that a queen old enough to demonstrate her value as a breeder, will be superseded shortly after her introduction into a strange colony.

Queens that have been laying heavily suffer seriously from the confinement in a small cage and the journey through the mails. Often they will never do as well for the buyer as they have done previously, and he is inclined to feel that he has not been treated fairly. As a rule, the same money invested in young untested queens, will bring far better results to the buyer, as well as being better for the seller. If a half dozen young queens are purchased from a breeder with good stock, at least one of them is quite likely to prove excellent. The best queen that the author ever has known he secured as an untested queen at a nominal price. There is probably no extensive queen rearing yard which would part with as good a queen for fifty dollars after she had demonstrated her value. In fact, she would not be for sale at any price, for she would be too valuable as a breeder. Yet the chances are that, after she had demonstrated her ability by outdoing everything else in the apiary for three successive seasons, she would be superseded within a few weeks after being sent through the mails.

Buyers should bear in mind that old queens which have laid heavily for one or more seasons, cannot be expected to repeat their former performances after a journey by mail. Such queens can only be shipped safely on combs in a nucleus, where they can continue laying lightly for some time. Someone has compared the sudden checking of the work of a laying queen, with the shipment of a cow, which is a heavy milker, without drawing her milk for several days. Neither can be expected to be as good again.

CHAPTER XII

The Introduction of Queens.

In order to be successful in the introduction of queens, it is necessary to overcome the antagonism of the colony toward a stranger. It must be borne in mind that, normally, a strange bee will be recognized as an enemy or a robber and at once driven out or killed. In order that the queen be welcomed as a member of the community, it is necessary that she be permitted to acquire the colony odor, and that she become somewhat familiar with her new surroundings so that she will not manifest, by her own excitement, the fact that she is a stranger. There are many indications of the colony odor and, in the absence of proof to the contrary, it is safe to assume that the bees depend upon this common odor as a means of identification of the members of the community.

There are many different methods of introduction of queens, which are followed with greater or lesser degrees of success. All these methods may be divided into two classes: those which depend upon the confinement of the queen until she acquires the common characteristics of the hive, as the cage methods; and those which create such an abnormal condition and so much confusion in the hive, that the undue excitement of one or more individuals will not be noticed, as the smoke or other direct methods.

Under the first plan, the bees are at first antagonistic to the new queen, which is recognized as a stranger, but are unable to reach her because of the barrier furnished by the screen covering the cage. After a time the bees recognize the fact that no other queen is present in the hive, the antagonism disappears, and she is accepted as the natural mother of the community.

Under any method in the second class, the colony is thrown into a state of excitement and uproar, to such an extent that the agitation and fear manifested by the new queen, upon finding herself in a strange hive, will not be apparent to the bees, since they are also in a state of confusion. By the time the excitement subsides, the foreign odor of the new queen will no longer be apparent, and she will settle down to the business of egg lay-ing as though she had always been present in the hive. By this method it is the usual way to remove the old queen either shortly before or just at the time the new queen is introduced.

Details of Cage Methods.

All the variations of the cage method are comparatively simple. The old queen is first removed from the hive and the

new one is introduced in a cage, Figure 37. Probably the safest method of all is the one where the queen is

Fig. 37.   The Miller introducing cage.

placed alone in a cage that covers a small patch of emerging brood. The emerging bees are, of course, friendly enough, and within two or three days she will be laying in her small enclosure and surrounded by a small group of attendants who found her present when they emerged. The cage is then carefully removed, and the comb replaced in the hive with as little disturbance as possible. Such a cage is made with a piece of ordinary wirecloth about four inches square, sometimes smaller. Each of the four corners is cut away for about three quarters of an inch. The four sides are then bent down, forming a wire box open at the bottom. The queen is placed under this and the wire pressed into the comb. It is well to have a few cells of sealed honey inside the cage, although the bees are likely to feed the queen through the meshes of the cage. When this plan is used in a hive where no brood is present, some newly emerged workers should be placed in the cage with the queen. The attitude of the bees toward the queen will determine when it is safe to release her. If on opening the hive, the cage is found to be covered with a tight cluster of bees, she would be balled immediately if released. When the bees are found to be paying but little attention to her presence, it is usually safe to remove the cage.

The Benton mailing cages are stocked with candy before the queens are confined. Usually there will be quite a little of this candy still left, at the time the queens are to be introduced. If so, all that is necessary is to remove the old queen, remove the paper across the exit hole which is filled with candy, and leave it to the bees to remove the candy, and release the queen. It is likely to require from one to three days to remove the candy, and by that time, there is little danger to the new queen. If but little candy remains, the paper should be left over the hole for a day or two before removing. When the paper is removed, if the candy is almost gone, a little broken comb honey may be pushed into the cavity. Bees are likely to be friendly to the queen which has been caged in the hive for two days, and the bees which remove the honey are likely to gorge themselves to the point of quietude.

Some beekeepers by going to a little extra trouble, insure

Fig. 38. A Mississippi queen-rearing apiary.

success by this method. When new queens are ordered they cage the old queens in the hive until the newcomers arrive. The old queens are then destroyed, and the new ones placed in the same cages and replaced in the same hives. The cages have already acquired the hive odors, and the bees have become accustomed to the presence of their queens in the cages. By the time the candy has been removed, there is a very small element of danger.

Direct Introduction.

The easiest time for direct introduction of queens is during a heavy honeyflow. At such a time the bees will be in a constant state of activity because of the wealth of honey coming in, and queens can be introduced with a minimum of danger. At such times, the author has gone to the hives to be requeened, caught the old queens and run in the new ones, with little effort to disarrange the affairs of the community, yet the plan worked with entire success with colony after colony. Many of the direct methods which are so successful during a honeyflow, must be followed very carefully under other conditions, or failure will result.

There are several of the direct methods, familiarly known as smoke method, flour method, water, and honey methods, etc. The same principle underlies them all. In every case the object is to develop such an abnormal condition within the hive, that the change of queens can be made without the fact being discovered by the bees.

The smoke method has recently been exploited as something new. Some of the details of the practice are all that is new, for Alley described a similar way of introducing queens by means of tobacco smoke as long ago as 1885. He directed as follows:

"When tobacco smoke is used to introduce them, throw some grass against the entrance to keep the smoke in and the bees from coming out. Blow in a liberal amount of smoke, and then let the queen run in at the top through the hole used for the cone-feeder."

The method as advocated by A. C. Miller does not anticipate the use of tobacco, but the ordinary smoke always available to the beekeeper with a lighted smoker. He describes his plan as follows:

"A colony to receive a queen has the entrance reduced to about a square inch with whatever is convenient, as grass, weeds, rags or wood, and then about three puffs of thick white smoke—because such smoke is safe—is blown in and the entrance closed. It should be explained that there is a seven-eighths inch space below the frames, so that the smoke which is blown in at the entrance, readily spreads and penetrates to all parts of the hive. In from fifteen to twenty seconds the colony will be roaring. The small space at the entrance is now opened; the queen is run in, followed by a gentle puff of smoke, and the entrance again closed and left closed for about ten minutes, when it is reopened, and the bees allowed to ventilate and quiet down. The full entrance is not given for an hour or more, or even until the next day."

Neither of the smoke methods above given, nor, for that matter, most of the direct methods, are entirely reliable under adverse conditions. The great advantage in the use of such a method is the saving in time. Some queen breeders of the author's acquaintance have used the smoke method extensively for this reason, and with good success. Introducing a queen which is taken from a hive or nucleus and given at once to anoth-

Fig. 39. A queen-rearing apiary in Georgia.

er, is a much simpler matter than the introduction of a queen which has been caged for a week and probably travelled several hundred miles in a mailbag, where she had opportunity to ac- quire all kinds of foreign odors. The experienced man will soon learn when he can with safety depend upon a short cut, and when there is danger in doing so.

Honey and Flour Methods.

These methods are similar except that in one case honey is used and in the other case flour is the medium. The honey method is used with good success in introducing virgins to bees in packages, after they have been confined for a few hours. The queen is simply dropped into a cup of honey and entirely submerged in it, and then dropped in among the bees, which at once proceed to clean her up. For introducing queens into full colonies, this plan does not always succeed.

Where the queen is covered with flour, she may be accepted or not, depending much upon other conditions. Where the honey method is used, the queen is much more likely to be accepted if the honey in which she is dipped is taken from the hive to which she is to be given, at the time of her introduction.

Water Method.

This method requires a little more trouble, but is generally successful according to reports, and also according to the auth- or's experience. The bees are shaken from the combs, and sprinkled with water until they are soaking wet. The new queen is wet likewise and dropped on the pile of wet bees in the bottom of the hive. The combs are then replaced and the hive covered.

Neither of these methods is attractive, since it hardly seems like proper treatment to give a valuable queen.

Introduction of Virgins.

A newly emerged queen while she is still downy, say within half an hour of the time of her emergence, can be run into any queenless colony or nucleus with safety. The bees are apparently conscious that any bee of such a tender age is incapable of harm, and she is accepted as a child of the community For such, it is not necessary to provide any artificial stimulus of any kind; smoke, flour, or water are all unnecessary.

Virgins that are four or five days old are more difficult to introduce, than are fertile queens. Alley recommended dipping the virgin in honey, thinned with a little water as above described, and then dropping her into the queenless hive. He wrote that virgins could only be introduced successfully to colonies that had been queenless for at least three days. It has often been advised to leave colonies queenless for this period before introducing fertile queens, but the author prefers to give a fertile queen immediately on removing the old queen. With virgins there is a larger element of danger.

CHAPTER XIII

Spreading Disease from the Queen Yard.

It is an unfortunate fact that much of the responsibility for the present wide-spread prevalence of foulbrood must be laid at the door of the careless queen breeder. Foulbrood has been introduced into many localities by the purchase of queens from diseased apiaries. The queen breeder cannot use too much care in keeping his apiary and his locality free from disease. In any event, queens should not be mailed to purchasers from an apiary where disease is present. In our present state of knowledge of European foulbrood, it is uncertain in just what manner the disease is spread, but it is very probable that a queen bee, taken from a diseased colony, might be the means of introducing it into a healthy colony, even though no honey or bees accompany her.

It is reasonably certain that there is little danger of the spread of American foulbrood, except in the honey from diseased colonies. The postal regulation which requires that honey used to make candy, to stock queen cages to be sent through the mails, be boiled for thirty minutes, is supposed to meet all requirements. While this may be true, as far as American foulbrood is concerned, it is not sufficient protection for the purchaser, from European foulbrood or paralysis.

The late O. O. Poppleton related something of his experience with paralysis, to the writer. For a time he had serious losses among his bees from this disease. He was finally able to trace the trouble to the introduction of queens from the yards of a well known breeder. By requeening all his yards with a different strain of bees, he was able to eliminate the disease. Later he introduced the same disorder to his apiaries again with queens from another source. On investigating the matter, he was surprised to learn that the man from whom he bought

the new lot of queens, had previously purchased a breeding
queen from the breeder from whom he had first contracted the
disease.   It accordingly became necessary to requeen his apiaries
with new stock, a second time, to get rid of paralysis.

Diseases of adult bees are, as yet, but little understood;
but it is quite probable that there are several different diseases,
all of which are known under the general name of paralysis.
It is very evident that this trouble, whatever its nature, is
widely disseminated by the sale of queens and bees in packages.
The trouble has long been prevalent in the south, especially
in Florida, but, of late, it is becoming common in many northern
localities.   It has attracted special notice in Wisconsin and
Washington.   In dry and warm seasons it is not serious, but in
cold and damp summers becomes a serious problem.

Cases have been called to the writer's attention, where
all the bees introduced from a certain locality have died with

Fig. 40. A Minnesota queen yard.

this disorder, while the stock which had previously been present in the apiary remained in healthy condition.

If the business of queen breeding is to remain permanent and profitable, it is highly desirable that concerted action be taken, looking to the control of shipment of queens or bees from diseased apiaries. The buyer should be assured that he will not endanger his future prospects by buying queens anywhere that they are offered. About the only solution that seems readily apparent is federal supervision of queen yards. An increasing number of expert beekeepers are being employed in the extension service of the United States department, and these could be used to inspect all queen-breeding apiaries at least once each year, in connection with their other work.

Several of the states have provision for the inspection of queen-breeding apiaries, and withhold certificates of health from apiaries where disease is found. However, not all the states have inspection and those that have do not have uniform regulations. The shipment of both bees and queens is becoming so general that uniform interstate regulations are very desirable.

In the opinion of the author, the future of the business depends very much on the attitude which the queen breeders, as a class, assume toward this question.

Books On Beekeeping For Sale by the American Bee Journal

LANGSTROTH ON THE HONEY BEE

REVISED BY DADANT.

THIS book originally written by Rev. L. L. Langstroth, the inventor of the movable frame hive, has been revised and kept up to date by the editor of the American Bee Journal. It is the one book that no beekeeper can afford to ·be without. It contains careful and accurate accounts of the life and habits of the honey bee and the mysteries of the hive. Full and reliable information concerning the detection and treatment of disease, the sources of nectar and pollen, and the care of the apiary throughout the year are included. The best methods of producing and marketing large crops of honey are made clear. This book is nicely bound in attractive cloth cover and contains 575 pages. The price is very low for a book of the size and quality. Sent postpaid for $1.50, or with the American Bee Journal one year both for only $2.50. Canada postage, 15 cents extra. It is published in 3 foreign languages, French, Spanish and Russian, at a slightly advanced price.

1,000 QUESTIONS ABOUT BEES

ANSWERED BY DR. C. C. MILLER.

FOR many years Doctor Miller has conducted the question and answer department in The American Bee Journal. During that time he has answered questions relating to every phase of beekeeping. These questions have been sifted and arranged by M. G. Dadant and are now offered in book form.

No matter what your problem is, you will find the answer in this book, for beekeepers of all ages and all stages of experience have brought their queries to Doctor Miller. This book is intended to supplement the regular text books on beekeeping, and will be an invaluable aid to every beekeeper, whether he be a novice or an expert.

The texts tell a connected story of bee life and the principles of honey production, while this takes up singly the many questions that confront the beekeeper in his everyday practice in the apiary. Dozens of subjects not mentioned in the ordinary text and special angles of many other subjects which have been overlooked elsewhere are taken up and made clear by the most popular writer on beekeeping.

Should be included in every list of bee books.

Attractive cloth cover; 200 pages; $1.25.

As a premium with The American Bee Journal. Price with one year's subscription, $2.00. Canadian postage 15 cents extra.

Books On Beekeeping For Sale by the American Bee Journal

PRODUCTIVE BEE-KEEPING

BY FRANK C. PELLETT

ONE of the latest text books on bee-keeping, by the former State Apiarist of Iowa and Staff correspondent of The American Bee Journal, as its name indicates, is a book for the practical man. Easily understood by the beginner, it covers the field of practical honey production very fully and is a valuable book of reference for the extensive honey producer. The author enjoys a wide acquaintance among leading beekeepers of the United States and Canada and has described the systems of management which are successfully employed under a wide range of conditions. The best methods have been studied, sifted and excellently arranged.

A Lippincott Farm Manual, 134 illustrations, 320 pages.

CONTENTS—

1. Beekeeping a Fascinating Pursuit.
2. The Business of Beekeeping.
3. Making a Start With Bees.
4. Arrangement of the Apiary.
5. Sources of Nectar.
6. The Occupants of the Hive.
7. Increase.
8. Feeding.
9. Production of Comb Honey.
10. Production of Extracted Honey.
11. Wax, A By-Product.
12. Diseases and Enemies of Bees.
13. Wintering.
14. Marketing the Honey Crop.
15. Laws That Concern the Bee-keeper.

Durable cloth binding. Price, $1.75, postpaid.
With American Bee Journal, 1 year, $2.50.

FIRST LESSONS IN BEEKEEPING
BY C. P. DADANT.

FOR many years a book under the above title has been in the market. It w s originally written by Thos. G. Newman, and later revised by C. P. Dadant.

While the present book bears the same title, it is entirely new and has been rewritten from beginning to end. Even though you have the old book, you will want the new one also, for it is a far better book than the old one ever was, and it is right up to date.

The senior editor of The American Bee Journal, who is the author of the New First Lessons, has spent nearly all his life in a beekeeping atmosphere. His father, the late Charles Dadant, was an investigator who became well known on both sides of the Atlantic, and whose writings have been translated into several languages. As a young man the author of First Lessons was associated with his father in honey production and assisted him in the many experiments which he conducted in his efforts to make beekeeping a practical business.

Of late Mr. Dadant has traveled extensively, both in Europe and America, and is familiar with the best methods of honey production and with the leading beekeepers of many countries. With a lifetime of practical experience and such unusual opportunities for observation, C. P. Dadant is especially fitted to prepare a book for the beginning beekeeper.

Just the things you want to know, in a style easily understood, and with many pictures to explain the text.

You may safely recommend First Lessons in Beekeeping to your friends.

200 pages, cloth, fully illustrated. Price, postpaid, **$1.00. With the** American Bee Journal, 1 year $1.75. Canadian postage 15 cents extra.

American Bee Journal, Hamilton, Illinois

CPSIA information can be obtained
at www.ICGtesting.com
Printed in the USA
BVOW10s0757190217
476483BV00007B/56/P